# Coaching
# Young
# Performers

**sports coach UK** is the brand name of The National Coaching Foundation
and has been such since April 2001

ISBN-13: 978-1-902523-56-3
ISBN-10: 1-902523-56-3

**First edition**
Author: Martin Hagger
Editors: Anne Simpkin, Penny Crisfield
Sub-editor: Stuart Biddle
Designer: Debbie Backhouse

**Second edition**
Author: Chris Earle
Editor: Nicola Craine
Sub-editor: Warwick Andrews
Designer: Julia King

Cover photo courtesy of actionplus sports images
All other photos courtesy of **sports coach UK** and actionplus sports images

**sports coach UK** would like to thank Lyn Goodliffe for her valuable input
into the second edition

Coachwise Business Solutions

**sports coach UK**
114 Cardigan Road
Headingley
Leeds LS6 3BJ
Tel: 0113-274 4802
Fax: 0113-275 5019
Email: coaching@sportscoachuk.org
Website: www.sportscoachuk.org

Patron: HRH The Princess Royal

Published on behalf of **sports coach UK** by
**Coachwise Business Solutions**
Coachwise Ltd
Chelsea Close
Off Amberley Road
Armley
Leeds LS12 4HP
Tel: 0113-231 1310
Fax: 0113-231 9606
Email: enquiries@coachwisesolutions.co.uk
Website: www.coachwisesolutions.co.uk

Coaches play a vital role in the development of young performers at all levels. Their influence is crucial in shaping not only potential elite performers, but also future generations of active, healthy individuals.

Research has shown that it takes up to ten years to produce an elite performer. It could be argued that it takes as long, if not longer, to produce quality coaches who understand how to develop children both as athletes and as active, healthy individuals. This resource is designed to help coaches adapt their coaching sessions to meet the needs of young performers. Covering topics such as how children develop physically and emotionally, and how they learn and improve skill, it aims to show coaches how to apply their knowledge and provide positive sporting experiences for young performers. More specifically, this resource should help coaches to:

- recognise the importance of taking a long-term approach to the development of young performers in sport

- explain why children and young people take part in sport

- plan and deliver sessions and programmes to meet the needs of young performers

- recognise the effects of the chronological, developmental and training ages[1] of young performers, and how these will affect their aspirations in sport

- follow good practice when coaching young performers

- identify and accommodate the needs of young elite performers.

Within each chapter there are some questions or thought-provoking suggestions to help coaches relate some of the information to their own coaching experiences. There are also information panels to help coaches focus their attention on important themes and issues when coaching young performers. In addition, specific recommendations regarding coaching practices and styles are made with reference to different stages of development.

1   See page 1 for definitions of training ages.

*Throughout this resource, the pronouns he, she, him, her and so on are interchangeable and intended to be inclusive of both males and females. It is important in sport, as elsewhere, that both genders have equal status and opportunities.*

# Contents

# CHAPTER ONE: Introduction

Many children and young people are involved in sport. Coaches can help their development as performers and as people. Young performers, in the context of this resource, are children and young people who may simply enjoy participating in sport or who may also have performance ambitions. Some may even have the desire to be among the best in their sport (referred to in this resource as *young elite performers*). Whatever the talents or ambitions of young performers, coaches need to be able to respond to them to ensure their experiences of sport are positive.

Throughout this resource, certain terms are used to describe children and young people. It is important to clarify how these are used as they can sometimes be interpreted differently. The following text and table explains the common usage of terms in this book. The age ranges associated with these are only a guide as children of the same age can be at very different stages of development.

The term **children** usually refers to anyone up to the age of 16. The stage at which children become young

| Terminology | Average age range (in years) |
| --- | --- |
| Young children | 7–10s |
| Pre-adolescents | 10–12s |
| Early adolescents | 12–14s |
| Late adolescents | 14–16s |
| Post-adolescents | 16+ |

people will depend on when they go through adolescence and mature. However, as a general guide, **young people** can refer to anyone over the age of 16. Children and young people can differ from one another in terms of their:

- **chronological age** – their actual age in years

- **developmental age** – the extent to which their emotional, physical or social development compares, exceeds or falls short of that of a typical child of that age

- **training age** – the number of years' experience they may have gained through regular, structured training.

All these factors need to be considered when coaches are planning and taking sessions to suit the needs of their performers.

By the end of this chapter, you should be able to:

- identify why you coach children and young people
- explain why children and young people are different to adults
- describe how to adapt the coaching process to meet the needs of young performers
- describe the difference between chronological, developmental and training age
- explain your additional responsibilities to young performers
- explain how lifestyle factors affect young performers.

## 1.0 Why Coach Young Performers?

Coaching young performers can be extremely rewarding. They are usually very keen to participate in sporting activities, and explore, demonstrate and develop their abilities. They are also, potentially, the sports stars of tomorrow. A survey conducted for the Swedish Sports Federation (Allert, 1996) concluded that it had taken an average of 5500 hours to produce Sweden's top international performers (ie $3\frac{1}{2}$ hours of training a day, for $5\frac{1}{2}$ days a week, for 48 weeks a year, for 6 years). According to other researchers (Bloom 1985, Ericsson et al, 1993 & 1994), the process can take even longer – approximately ten years or 10,000 hours of extensive practice and preparation. Research findings such as these illustrate the long-term effort and commitment required to produce elite performers.

The implications for coaches are obvious – short-term results and performances are not important for young performers in the context of their overall long-term athletic development; it is vital to take a long-term view.

Whether young performers are elite, advanced, intermediate, recreational or beginner, coaches not only have the opportunity to prepare them to attain their goals in competition, but can also ensure that their experiences of sport are both satisfying and enjoyable.

Coaching young performers is very challenging. It requires a great deal of thought, preparation and knowledge on the part of the coach. A specialist and intricate knowledge of their sport is essential if coaches are to make the best decisions for their young performers. For example, some sports such as gymnastics and swimming may require intensive training and practice from a very young age.

Finally, the impact that coaching has on young performers will go beyond the sport itself. It will help them to develop in other areas such as interpersonal relationships, academic work and other interests. Most coaches appreciate this and make every effort to recognise the effect sport and coaching may have on their performers' lifestyles beyond practice and training.

## 1.1 Why Young Performers are Different to Adults

Young performers are a special population with whom coaches have additional responsibilities above and beyond those when coaching mature performers. Coaches also have a duty of care in terms of protection and guidance in the absence of young performers' parents[1] or guardians. Young performers up to the age of 18 are still developing and, depending on

their sport, may well not reach their potential until they are more mature. Their development must never be compromised. It is essential that coaches know the extent of their young performers' abilities and bear these in mind when they plan sessions and programmes.

Coaches should:

- adapt sessions according to young performers' chronological, developmental and training ages
- provide sessions which are stimulating and challenging for young performers
- provide sessions which are fun and enjoyable, particularly for younger children
- listen to young performers and accommodate their needs.

1   The use of the term *parents* in this resource implies both parents and carers.

Coaches also need to protect themselves against liability or allegations which could cause conflict between them, the performer and the parent. They must ensure they do not put themselves in a position which may inadvertently threaten or upset young performers and should therefore:

- avoid shouting and derogatory comments

- use positive comments and feedback whenever possible

- keep physical contact to a minimum unless absolutely necessary

NB When contact is necessary, make sure there is at least one other adult present – as there can be different guidelines for different sports, make sure you know what the national governing body (NGB) for your sport advises.

- treat all young performers equally to avoid favouritism

- be non-judgemental when talking to young performers

- empathise with young performers and be aware of their emotions.

## Children and young people are not just mini-adults

Just because children and young people are smaller in stature does not necessarily mean they will be able to cope with scaled-down adult prescriptions for sport.

Coaches must acknowledge the additional demands on their coaching skills and adapt their coaching to meet the long-term needs of young performers.

- **Make it fun**

  Young performers vote with their feet. If they don't enjoy a coaching session, it is highly unlikely they will want to return and more likely that they will find something else to do – perhaps something less active which encourages a sedentary lifestyle. Coaches should therefore provide a fun, challenging and creative environment for young performers.

- **Avoid specialising too early**

  Specialising in a particular sport too early is likely to lead to *burnout* (Harsanyi, 1985). Coaches should therefore develop young performers' all-round athletic skills and abilities first. Then, when these have been mastered, they should consider how they can help young performers to maximise their sporting potential, or encourage them to become regular participants in physical activity.

- **Put young performers first**

  Too many competitions and inappropriate training when young can lead to under-achievement in physical, tactical, technical and mental abilities later on. A well-planned, long-term strategy needs to be adopted by governing bodies, coaches, teachers, parents and the young performers themselves to ensure that coaching programmes maximise potential and promote regular adherence to an active and healthy lifestyle.

## Young performers are changing all the time

Coaches should appreciate that young performers do not differ from one another only because of different chronological ages, they differ in their developmental and training age as well[1].

Children and young people of a given chronological age can differ by up to two years in terms of their developmental age. Therefore a boy or girl of eleven may have the physique of a nine-year-old or a 13-year-old. Coaches should also note that young performers with a great deal of experience and training will be able to progress relatively quickly compared with those who have little or no background in these areas.

There are many elements to development and these are manifest in children in different ways. Physical developmental factors may limit young performers in terms of coping with the demands of a task, but their rate of improvement will increase as they develop. Psychological development, however, will affect young performers' behaviour and attitudes in different ways and is influenced by various factors (eg gender differences, rate of maturity, innate characteristics and peer influences). Coaches may, in some cases, find it necessary to group young performers by developmental and training age as opposed to chronological age.

## Young performers have a tremendous capacity for learning

Children and young people are innately curious and have a natural inclination to explore the world around them. They have an active desire to learn and acquire new skills. Part of this need can be satisfied by taking part in sport and coaches can serve as facilitators in this process.

Young performers are very keen learners, provided they have the appropriate stimuli and guidance.

If they feel they are not accomplishing anything or that they are worthless, they can quickly lose interest. Therefore, the level and demands of the practice sessions need to be tailored to meet the needs and aspirations of young performers. Ideally, when the coach's influence is removed, children should still have a desire to learn more and continue their participation (see Chapter 3.4).

1   Definitions of training age, developmental age and chronological age can be found on page 1.

## Extra care for young performers

Some young performers may have a disability and/or additional needs. It is important coaches know what these are and how to accommodate them. For more information on coaching disabled people, the following **sports coach UK (scUK)** workshops and resources[1] are recommended:

- *How to Coach Disabled People in Sport*
- *Coaching Disabled Performers.*

In addition, Disability Sport England[2] and the English Federation of Disability Sport[3] can both provide guidance on disability issues in sport.

Regardless of their individual needs, however, children and young people are all vulnerable. They are often less familiar with surroundings and equipment than adults and are also less aware of their actions and consequences. As a result they require an extra duty of care above and beyond that of mature adult performers.

Coaches should therefore be responsible for:

- making young performers aware of potential hazards in the sport or task and checking their understanding
- creating a safe environment in which young performers can practise and train away from potential hazards (eg roads, hard surfaces)
- ensuring practices are supervised by an adult at all times
- teaching young performers safety drills so they are safe when they practise outside the coaching environment.

Coaches should also understand their legal responsibilities when coaching young performers. In particular they should follow good practice in terms of supervision and child protection. They need to recognise and carry out their responsibilities in child protection.

---

1 All workshop participants receive a complimentary copy of the resource. Further copies are available from **Coachwise 1st4sport** (tel 0113-290 7612 or visit www.1st4sport.com).

2 Tel 020-8801 4466 or visit www.disabilitysport.org.uk

3 Tel 0161-247 5294 or visit www.efds.net

This means they should be able to:

- respond appropriately to any children or young people who disclose that they are being abused

- know what to do if they have concerns that an adult may be abusing a child or young person

- conform to good practice guidelines to ensure the welfare of the child or young person is paramount and that their behaviour as a coach is not open to criticism.

Further information on the responsibilities and liabilities of coaching young performers can be gained from the **scUK** workshop *Good Practice and Child Protection* and its accompanying resource *Protecting Children: A Guide for Sportspeople*[1]. For more advice on the legal responsibilities of coaching, you are recommended to attend the **scUK** workshop *The Responsible Sports Coach.*

## 1.2 The Role of the Coach

The coach serves a number of important roles such as teacher, role model, mentor, carer and trainer. Good coaching does not mean telling performers what to do all the time. This may cause young performers to rely too heavily on their coach. While coaching does involve advising young performers on the training and activities they should be doing, it should also empower them to make decisions on their own and to be independent. This is particularly important as there will often be times when the coach is not present.

For more information on the role of a coach, the following **scUK** workshops and resources[2] are recommended:

- *What is Sports Coaching?*
- *Coaching Methods and Communication* workshop and its accompanying resource *The Successful Coach: Guidelines for Coaching Practice.*

---

1 and 2   All workshop participants receive a complimentary copy of the resource. Further copies are available from **Coachwise 1st4sport** (tel 0113-290 7612 or visit www.1st4sport.com).

## 1.3 Young Performers' Lifestyles

There are many factors which influence the lifestyles of young performers. This chapter explains each one and how it affects young performers in sport. Lifestyle factors include:

- friends
- family
- parents
- school
- other interests.

### Friends

Friends are important to children and young people especially as they enter their teenage years. The influence of friends may make young performers decide to continue their sport or give it up completely. Coaches should therefore provide opportunities for young performers to play with their friends, but also encourage them to mix with others and develop a passion for the sport itself.

Most young performers will not wish to sacrifice social aspects of their life entirely in favour of sport. Coaches should therefore encourage them to view sport as only part of their lives, just like school, family and social commitments. Young performers should be encouraged to recognise that their commitment to sport should reflect their ambitions. For those with high aspirations, coaches should reassure them that sacrificing other pleasures (eg spending time with their friends) can lead to more success and satisfaction from their sport. They should remind them of the rewards sport can offer and emphasise that they should not in any way feel ashamed of being dedicated to their sport and achieving success.

### Family

Families often plan to go away during school holiday periods. This means young performers may be obliged to take a break with their family and this will result in absence from training or practice. These periods need not necessarily be disruptive. If coaches make an effort to be aware of these holidays they can provide a schedule of practices or drills to help the performer maintain form and fitness during this time. Parents are often supportive of such contingency plans and can help the coach by supervising the practice during the holiday. Alternatively, a break in training or practice can be scheduled at the same time as the family holiday which can be equally beneficial.

Often children are not aware of the need for careful advance planning so the coach must make an effort to find out from performers or their parents when family holidays or other commitments are planned.

## Parents

In contrast to adults, young performers are usually under the care of their parents. Clearly, parents will have a significant influence on their child's beliefs about sport and without them many would not take part. For example, parents are usually responsible for financing children's participation in sport and for transporting them to and from various venues. Parents are often very enthusiastic about their child's participation and progress. They can form a valuable link between the coach and the young performer and assist the coach in getting messages across. For instance, they may help implement and supervise independent practices at home or reinforce the important points about technique, training or competitions that young performers may be expected to remember or attend. The coach should talk to parents or arrange times when they can meet as they can be a useful ally for the coach and are often very willing to help out.

Sometimes parental influences may be disruptive, for example, if they have different goals, frequently interfere during sessions, or put undue pressure on their child or the coach. It may be possible to alleviate some of these pressures during training sessions by allocating an area where parents can sit close enough to watch, but far enough away so as not to have an influence on the session. Coaches must be sensitive to both young performers and their parents, and encourage the right balance for the child in terms of parental support and child independence.

---

**TASK**

What would you say to parents if they asked if they could talk to their child to help them during one of your sessions?
Remember, you would want to talk to them in a calm and non-confrontational manner.

---

Sometimes, parents may want to get involved directly. For instance, they may tell their children what they think is best for them and the children may then bring these opinions to the practice session. Often coaches are competing with the advice of over-keen parents which may conflict with their own philosophy.

Alternatively, parents may tell the coach directly what they think is best for their child. Coaches can deal with these situations by establishing ground rules from the outset. They can remind parents that sending their child for coaching involves trusting the coach with the child's development as a sports performer and it is disruptive if other views are expressed. Coaches should make parents feel that their support is valuable. They can do this by sharing their coaching philosophy with parents and involve them in setting goals. Many parents will have constructive comments to make and coaches should encourage them to express these at suitable times (eg after the session).

In stark contrast to the above, coaches should also be aware that some young performers may not receive parental support or encouragement, even though they enjoy sport. It may be difficult for them to sustain participation for a variety of reasons (eg lack of transport, money), particularly if their parents see no value in them taking part in physical activity. There is no easy solution to situations like this and coaches therefore need to respond in a sensitive manner.

## School

All young performers are likely to be engaged in full-time education whether it be primary/secondary school or college of further education. This makes them a special case as school places demands on them which may affect their sports participation. School and college work is clearly important as it has implications for later life. For most young performers, sport should therefore complement school work and not cause any conflict.

Only the very best young performers can afford to commit a large proportion of their time to training. The coach must recognise the additional demands of school and adapt training or practice sessions accordingly. The school year follows a consistent pattern so coaches not only have the opportunity to plan their practice sessions around school hours but also to make adjustments for special periods such as examinations, school trips and holidays. This usually involves discussing school commitments with performers, their parents and possibly their teachers, so they can be worked into the training schedule. If coaches make an effort to do this, examinations and other school commitments will seem less of a disruption and it will help performers to cope better with the demands of sport and school.

Most schools should have a policy for dealing with gifted and talented pupils in all subject areas, including those who have been identified by NGBs or professional sports clubs. The policy should set out how the school will support the additional demands made on talented pupils by external sports organisations. This may include a flexible approach to curriculum delivery, timetabling of homework, provision of distance-learning packages, and selection of examinations.

Being sensitive to school commitments will help coaches and performers to set realistic goals. There is also less chance of creating conflict between school and sport, and this therefore should reduce the likelihood of young performers feeling pressurised to choose either one or the other to pursue.

### Other interests

Many young performers may well have other interests besides sport. It is important for coaches to know what these are and how they affect the lifestyle of young performers. For example, coaches might need to know:

- how committed the performers are to other activities

- how much time they spend on other activities

- where they rank their sport in terms of priorities with other activities

- whether the other activities complement sport (for instance, other sports may be useful cross-training and therefore can be built into the training programme).

This type of information will help coaches to understand where sport fits into the overall lifestyle of young performers. It will help them to gauge the appropriate intensity and frequency of practice sessions and be a useful guide to setting realistic goals.

## 1.4    Summary

Coaches should know why they coach young performers and be clear of their coaching philosophy towards them. They should recognise that young performers have special requirements and are dependent on their coach in many ways. Coaches should appreciate the different lifestyle demands of young performers and help them to balance these with their sporting activities. In particular, coaches should communicate effectively with the other people who have a major influence on young performers (ie parents, teachers and friends).

# CHAPTER TWO:
# Long-term Development

The success of performers at the highest level is widely acknowledged as a process that begins in childhood and which can take more than ten years to achieve. It relies on children valuing and enjoying the experience of physical activity. Coaches, teachers, sports leaders and, above all, parents, have a crucial role to play in these essential early stages of development.

Over the years, researchers have identified key factors which encourage children to become long-term participants of sport and to achieve their full potential. In recent years, Balyi's *Long-term Athlete Development (LTAD)* model has strongly influenced the attitudes of British sporting organisations to the development of performers.

By the end of this chapter, you should be able to:

- summarise key research relating to the long-term development of children

- describe the different stages of Balyi's LTAD model

- explain the benefits of long-term development

- recognise the implications of taking a long-term, performer-centred approach to coaching young performers.

## 2.0    Related Research

Bloom (1985) and Cote (1999) both devised three-stage models to describe the development of talented performers. Bloom's model (see Table 1 on page 14) focuses on the essential characteristics of performers, coaches and parents during each of the three stages of the talent development process.

Cote's model focuses on the influence of the family (see Table 2 on page 14). He challenges coaches to act in the best interests of young performers and to recognise their own limitations. This may mean specialising in just one of the three stages and recommending that young performers move to other coaches and/or clubs where appropriate coaching expertise and/or facilities are available.

*Table 1: Summary of Bloom's three-stage model*

|  | Early years | Middle years | Later years |
|---|---|---|---|
| **Performer** | • Joyful<br>• Playful<br>• Excited | • Wider perspective<br>• Committed<br>• Identity linked to sport | • Obsessed<br>• Responsible<br>• Consumed |
| **Coach** | • Kind<br>• Cheerful<br>• Focused on talent development process | • Strong leader<br>• Knowledgeable<br>• Demanding | • Successful<br>• Respected/feared<br>• Emotionally bonded |
| **Parent** | • Model work ethic<br>• Encouraging<br>• Supportive<br>• Positive | • Makes sacrifices<br>• Restricts own activities<br>• Child-centred | • Limited role<br>• Provides financial support |

*Table 2: Summary of Cote's three-stage model*

| Sampling years<br>Age 6–13 | Specialising years<br>Age 13–15 | Investment years<br>Post-15[1] |
|---|---|---|
| • Emphasis on fun and excitement<br>• Parents are key influence<br>• Need to sample a wide range of activities<br>• No sport-specific specialisation | • Focus on one or two sports<br>• Sport-specific skill development<br>• Practice time important<br>• Lifestyle management (balance of activities) | • Committed to achieving elite status in one sport<br>• Massive amount of practice time<br>• Family becomes a *sporting family* (ie family activities revolve around young person's sporting timetable) |

## 2.1    Long-term Athlete Development

Balyi's Long-term Athlete Development (LTAD) model promotes sport as a valuable activity which is enjoyable and which contributes to a healthy lifestyle. It encourages young people to participate in sport and provides opportunities for them to improve their skills and achieve their potential.

Balyi's earlier LTAD model consisted of four stages (see Table 3 on page 15).

1    If young performers go through the first two stages and are not talented, the investment stage describes their long-term adherence to physical activity.

*Table 3: Summary of Balyi's earlier LTAD model[1]*

| Stage | Age | Emphasis |
|---|---|---|
| 1: FUNdamentals | 6–10 | Emphasis on sampling a wide range of fun and creative sports activities in order to develop basic motor skills |
| 2: Training to Train | 10–13 (girls)/ 10–14 (boys) | Emphasis on applying basic skills and fitness to preferred sports/activities |
| 3: Training to Compete | 13–17 (girls)/ 14–18 (boys) | Emphasis on developing sport-specific skills, techniques, tactics and game strategies |
| 4: Training to Win | 17+ (girls)/ 18+ (boys) | Emphasis on specific training to achieve and maintain optimum performance at key competitions |

Many UK NGBs have adopted Balyi's model to help clarify levels and types of training and competition, and to develop clear performance pathways for their performers. As a result, the need for an additional stage (*Learning to Train*) between Stages 1 and 2 has been identified:

1  FUNdamentals
**2  Learning to Train**
3  Training to Train
4  Training to Compete
5  Training to Win.

In the original four-stage model, general and sport-specific skills are developed both towards the end of the *FUNdamental* stage and at the beginning of the *Training to Train* stage, resulting in an overlap.

In the five-stage version, there is no overlap between stages. This makes the LTAD process more effective and helps coaches to plan annual competition calendars more effectively.

The *Learning to Train* and *Training to Train* stages are crucial in the development of young performers. It is vital that coaches identify and rectify any skill or fitness deficits during these stages, as it will be difficult to do so later on.

The five-stage model is described in more detail in Table 4 on pages 16 to 17. Notice how the age ranges of the original four-stage model have been modified to incorporate the *Learning to Train* stage.

1   For further details, see Balyi, I (2002) **Long-term athlete development – the system and solutions.** *FHS.* Issue 14, pp6–9.

*Table 4: Modification of Balyi's original LTAD model*[1]

| Stage | Age | Summary |
|---|---|---|
| 1: FUNdamentals | 6–8 (girls)/ 6–9 (boys) | Probably the most important stage and, ironically and traditionally, the one in which more inexperienced coaches tend to be involved |
| 2: Learning to Train | 8–11 (girls)/ 9–12 (boys) | Stage lasts until peak growth spurt[2] immediately before start of menstruation (girls) and sexual development (boys). Age at which this occurs depends on genetic makeup rather than chronological age |
| 3: Training to Train | 11–14 (girls)/ 12–15 (boys) | Start of stage coincides with start of peak growth spurt[3] at beginning of adolescence and covers important period of physical and sexual development. A challenging stage for both performers and coaches |
| 4: Training to Compete | 14–17 (girls)/ 15–18 (boys) | End of stage coincides with age at which young performers become adults or seniors. Therefore probably the final stage in which coaches of young performers will be involved |
| 5: Training to Win | 17+ (girls)/ 18+ (boys) | Performers biologically mature and physical, technical, tactical and mental capacities fully developed |

1   For further details, see Balyi, I and Hamilton, A (2003) **Long-term athlete development update – trainability in childhood and adolescence.** *FHS.* Issue 20, pp6–8.

| Key Points |
| --- |

- Performers need to sample wide range of fun and creative activities
- No sport-specific specialisation
- Emphasis on development of basic motor skills, not competition
- Parents involved and supportive
- Tasks/groups set by biological rather than chronological age
- Speed, power and endurance developed using fun games
- No periodization

- Performers begin to apply basic skills and fitness to preferred activities
- Performers begin to reduce number of sports/activities
- Emphasis on learning how to train, **not** on outcome, but element of competition introduced (eg 25% of training programme)

- Individualised programmes required based on PHVs
- Teams split into groups of early, average and late maturers
- Girls and boys no longer train together
- Regular height checks (once a month; once a week at PHV) to help identify key periods for maximum training benefit and to avoid injuries
- Regular medical monitoring and musculo-skeletal screening of potentially talented young performers
- Excessive repetitive, weight-bearing aerobic work that may result in Osgood Schlatters' condition should be avoided. Non-weight-bearing exercises (eg swimming) recommended for young performers experiencing growing pains

- Fitness components need to be trained all year round, along with sport-specific skills, techniques, tactics and game strategies
- Sport-specific training for 1–2 hours, 9–12 times per week depending on event and training component
- Performers likely to have annual training and competition programme that allows them to reach peak performance twice a year (double periodised year = 2 x 24 week cycles) with a maximum of approximately 12 competitions per cycle (depending on the individual and the sport)
- Continued medical monitoring and musculo-skeletal screening
- Over-training and over-competition must be avoided

- Most performers train and compete on full-time basis
- Emphasis on specific training to achieve and maintain optimum performance at key competitions

2 and 3    Sometimes referred to as Peak Height Velocity (PHV).

Table 5 below shows how England Netball has applied the modified version of Balyi's LTAD model to the development of young netballers.

## Table 5: LTAD in netball

| FUNdamentals | Learning to Train | Training to Train | Training to Compete | Training to Win |
|---|---|---|---|---|
| Fun and participation | Introduce general physical conditioning | Emphasis on general physical conditioning | Sport- and individual-specific physical conditioning | Maintenance (or possible improvements) of physical capacities |
| General. Overall development of athleticism, agility, balance, coordination and speed | Fundamental technical skills introduced | Fundamental technical skills progressed to more specific skills | Sport-specific technical and playing skills under competitive conditions | Further development of technical, tactical and playing skills |
| Introduction to simple skills via modified game | Fundamentals of tactical work | Simple unit skills introduced | Advanced unit skills introduced | Modelling all aspects of training and performance |
| Participation in complementary sports (similar energy systems and movement pattern requirements) | Participation in complementary sports (similar energy systems and movement pattern requirements) | Tactical work extended | Advanced tactical preparation | Frequent prophylactic breaks |
| Speed and endurance through fun and games | Proper running, jumping and throwing techniques | Individualisation of fitness and technical training | Individualisation of technical/ tactical skills | All aspects of training individualised |
| Own body exercises for strength | Medicine ball, Swiss ball and own body exercises for strength and power | Extend mental skills by implementation | Test mental skills in competition | Social-psychology and team dynamics |
| Introduction to all positions | Introduction to mental training | Fundamentals of ancillary capacities | Sport- and individual-specific ancillary capacities | Fine-tune ancillary capacities |
| No periodization | Training for all positions | Area-specific training | Position-specific fitness and technical/tactical training | Double or multiple periodization |
| Participation in other sports | Single periodization | Single periodization | Double periodization | Netball-specific technical, tactical and fitness training nine to twelve times per week |
| | Netball-specific training up to four times per week with participation in other sports encouraged | Netball-specific training up to five times per week with participation in other sports encouraged | Netball-specific technical, tactical and fitness training six to nine times per week | |

## 2.2    Benefits of LTAD

Following the five-stage model promotes sport as a valuable activity which is enjoyable and which contributes to a healthy lifestyle. It encourages young people to participate in sport and provides opportunities for them to improve their skills and achieve their potential. Figure 1 below illustrates the three main, inter-linked outcomes of LTAD:

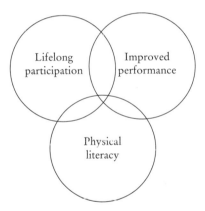

*Figure 1: Key outcomes of LTAD*

It is important for parents, teachers and coaches to work together with under-12s to develop their *physical literacy*. This means ensuring that young performers:

- master fundamental motor skills
- value physical education and sport
- are encouraged to participate in as many different sports as possible.

By doing so, young performers are more likely to become long-term participants in healthy, physical activity and to maximise their potential.

## 2.3    Implications for Coaching

Each of the five stages of LTAD challenges coaches to place young performers at the centre of all their planning, motivations and goals, and to always consider their best long-term interests. The first three stages are particularly relevant to coaching young performers. These focus on the development of general athletic skills – turning them into athletes first, then performers.

actionplus

Key conclusions to be drawn from Balyi's model include:

- Young performers develop at different rates. In particular, boys usually mature later than girls.

- Coaches should devise individual training and competition programmes according to biological/development rather than chronological age, particularly when working with performance-orientated[1] young performers.

- Although all biological systems are trainable, there are sensitive periods when appropriate training can accelerate and maximise the speed, strength and aerobic capacity of young performers. Failure to capitalise on these periods may result in a long-term deficit that young performers can never fully recover from (ie they will never maximise their potential).

## 2.4    Summary

Coaches should recognise the importance of taking a long-term, performer-centred approach to coaching young performers. It is essential that all-round athletic skills are developed before young performers are encouraged to specialise in specific sports. Once this has been achieved, coaches should devise individual training and competition programmes to ensure that the sporting potential of young performers is maximised. To do this effectively, coaches need to have a specialist knowledge of child development and of its implications for coaching. They should also communicate and cooperate with others involved in the talent development process (eg parents, teachers).

Further information on talent identification and young elite performers is provided in Chapter Six (pages 70 to 81).

---

1    Young performers who have either been identified as potential elite performers by NGBs, or whose commitment to training and competition is greater than the average young performer.

# CHAPTER THREE:
# Psychological and Social Development

Children and young people have a number of different reasons for taking part in sport. The focus of this chapter is primarily on how these motives affect children and young people in sport. An understanding of these motives will help coaches to get the best from their young performers.

By the end of this chapter, you should be able to:

- explain reasons why children and young people take part in sport
- explain how and why these reasons might change
- develop your young performers' competence and independence
- encourage fair play.

## 3.0 Why do Children and Young People Take Part in Sport?

Children and young people will have various reasons for taking part in sport. Their main reasons are:

- for pleasure and enjoyment
- for friendship and acceptance (eg to be with their friends)

- to demonstrate competence and independence to themselves and others
- for a sense of achievement (eg competition, self-improvement and self-esteem)
- for health and fitness.

Pleasure and enjoyment are perhaps the most important of these factors as they tend to be the common reasons why people participate in sport. For young performers, fun and enjoyment can arise from doing the sport itself for its inherent pleasures but also through achieving other outcomes such as improved performance, friendship or health. The participation of children and young people in sport can be affected by other factors (eg their stage of development, the influence of peers). This chapter will explain further how their reasons for engaging in sport can change over time.

## 3.1 Developing Competence

Children demonstrate an enormous capacity to learn about their environment from a very early age.

When interested in an object, infants will engage in unstructured play with that object. For instance, they will try to perform a task in a number of different ways to achieve the same outcome. This is the beginning of satisfying the need for competence.

Children and young people like to feel they can take action to influence their surroundings and demonstrate their ability to solve a task on their own or in front of others. Until the age of about ten years old, their need for competence is primarily intrinsic (ie children try to demonstrate to themselves that they can do certain movements). At approximately ten years old, children begin to develop the desire to demonstrate competence to others, particularly their friends. For teenagers up to about 14 years, competition and success in sport becomes more important and this can be damaging if they feel they are not as competent as their friends. For this age group, the coach should therefore attempt to match abilities and try to provide personal rather than comparative goals. Girls and boys may also differ in terms of how they develop competence. For instance, as they develop, some girls may be inclined to think that sport is unfeminine and they are not able to cope with the physical demands. From about the age of 14 to 18, children and young people become better equipped for competition and should therefore be encouraged to compete at an appropriate level where they can successfully demonstrate their skill. Table 6 on page 23 shows how young performers of different stages of development perceive competence.

*Table 6: How young performers perceive or develop competence, independence and effort/ability with action points for coaches*

| Age Group | Competence – being good at a sport | Independence – doing things for themselves | Perceptions of Effort and Ability | Action Points for Coaches |
|---|---|---|---|---|
| Young children | • Try to see how they can master skills for themselves.<br>• Quickly tire and move on if they are unsuccessful. | • Like to try things out and practise on their own even if they are unsuccessful.<br>• Can tire easily of monotonous tasks. | Have difficulty seeing the difference between effort and ability. | Coaches should:<br>• provide varied, less physically demanding practices<br>• encourage children to put as much effort in as they want. |
| Pre-adolescents | • Often form friendships due to common competences.<br>• Become more concerned with being better than their peers or friends. | Become increasingly reliant on the coach especially when new techniques are being learnt. | Begin to realise that some try harder than others but fail to equate this with superior ability. | Coaches should:<br>• begin to see the differences in ability and discreetly match groups with equal ability<br>• make practices varied<br>• reward effort more overtly. |
| Early adolescents | • See competition as being more important.<br>• Can be easily discouraged if they see success in terms of being better than their friends. | • Become more conscious of peer groups.<br>• Seek more independent practice to appear competent in front of peers. | Recognise that some have more ability than others but realise that this can be countered by increased effort. | Coaches should:<br>• recognise peer groups and their influences<br>• provide competitive opportunities to suit all standards<br>• encourage a healthy balance between process (task) goals and outcome goals (winning). |
| Late adolescents and post-adolescents | Begin to select and engage in tasks in which they perceive themselves to be successful. | See independent practice as being vital to success in competition. | View effort as being the determinant of performance and ability as a more limiting factor. | Coaches should encourage performers to:<br>• train and practise alone<br>• participate in competitions if they enjoy competing. |

## 3.2 Setting Goals

Setting the appropriate goals for the young performer is a crucial part of coaching. This will ensure their practices have meaning and help satisfy their individual and group needs. Goals should adhere to the **SMART** principles (ie they should be specific, measurable, agreed, realistic and time phased). In addition, they should be tailored to meet the performer's lifestyle, commitment and ambitions.

The agreement of goals between coach and young performer is particularly important. Coaches have a role as a facilitator to help performers feel a sense of achievement and, in order to do this, they need to discuss, agree and record goals with them.

The performer's input is vital if the goal is to lead to maximum acceptance, activation and satisfaction. It will also have more meaning and assist in satisfying their desire for competence and independence.

Unlike adults, young performers have the added factor of experiencing changes as they mature. If developmental changes result in unexpected fluctuations in performance, young performers should be helped to understand why these occur. For instance, it may be difficult for young performers to comprehend why they may have won all their races at 12 years old but find this is not achievable two years later.

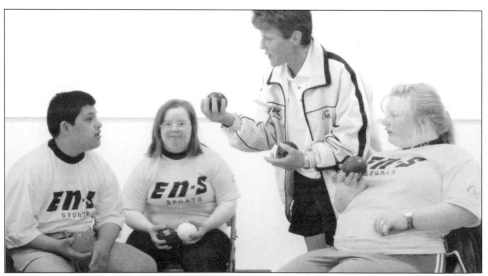

sports coach UK

In such circumstances, coaches should provide alternative goals which focus on personal improvement in order to maintain motivation, commitment and enjoyment.

There are two different types of goals – **outcome goals** (result-related, eg winning) and **process goals** (task-related, eg improving a technique). Outcome goals are commonly related to achievements in competition. These can clearly be very motivating if they are within reach, but can be detrimental if the performer is not likely to achieve them. Therefore coaches should also help young performers to appreciate the value in achieving goals, regardless of the outcome. Process goals can be set to help young performers focus on achieving or improving task-related aspects of their performance. For example, instead of trying to win a gymnastics competition, a performer may strive to improve the vault performance, particularly the landing as this was poor in the previous competition.

Process goals can come in many forms. They may be a low-level or practice competition, a time trial or even a specific training session which focuses the performer on one or two specific aspects of performance. They should be underpinned by the **SMART** principles and form part of a calendar programme which helps the performer and coach easily identify the proximity and timing of the short- and long-term goals.

Good process goals will ultimately help performers to achieve outcome goals – they can act as stepping stones to achieving the final goal. They do not focus on results and this helps to prevent performers from feeling demoralised if they do not win. For example, a performer may say: 'My vault performance was much better today – my landing was more controlled than in my previous performance'. If the performer had only set an outcome goal, the response might have been: 'I only came fifth again today'. This may obviously have a more negative effect[1].

---

1   For more information on types of goals and goal-setting, you are recommended to read the **scUK** resource *Coaching Sessions: A Guide to Planning and Goal-setting*, attend the **scUK** workshop *Goal-setting and Planning* and read its accompanying resource *Planning Coaching Programmes* (complimentary with the workshop). All **scUK** resources are available from **Coachwise 1st4sport** (tel 0113-201 5555 or visit www.1st4sport.com).

## 3.3    Motives and Motivation

Most young performers practise, train and compete in sport because they are motivated. Motivation can be viewed on a continuum ranging from extrinsic to intrinsic.

**Extrinsic motivation** is the activation or energy to perform an action to obtain an external reward. External rewards can be tangible like medals, trophies and certificates or intangible like praise and acknowledgement. An external reward is often incidental to the actual performance of the task (ie it is only obtained if a certain standard is met or if a person wins). For example, if performers engage in sport purely to gain a medal or receive praise from others, they are extrinsically motivated.

**Intrinsic motivation** is doing the sport for fun, enjoyment or pleasure gained from the sport or task itself. If performers feel happy and competent they have completed a sports task well without any reward, then they are intrinsically motivated. Encouraging young performers to be intrinsically motivated is desirable as they are more likely to persist at tasks even when they are not winning, receiving external rewards or praise from others, and therefore remain in the sport for longer.

Some young performers are highly motivated to take part in sport mostly for external rewards. Coaching a young performer who is extrinsically motivated can be less desirable because it tends to undermine more intrinsic reasons such as enjoyment or mastery of the task. External rewards, however, can be very motivating and positive, provided they are not the only motive for taking part in sport. For example, if a coach praises a performer for effort, the reward is informational rather than controlling (eg the reward informs the performer that the goal of putting in 100% effort has been achieved[1]).

Over-reliance on external rewards can lead to drop-out (see panel on page 27). For example, if external rewards are the only reason for competing and winning, young performers will most probably lose motivation to take part in sport if these are not achieved.

---

1    For more information, you are recommended to attend the **scUK** workshop *Motivation and Mental Toughness* and read its accompanying resource (complimentary with the workshop). All **scUK** resources are available from **Coachwise 1st4sport** (tel 0113-201 5555 or visit www.1st4sport.com).

Internal rewards, on the other hand, tend to be task-related and are more controllable (eg doing sport for satisfaction, competence and enjoyment). These are personal to the individual and, unlike external rewards, cannot be removed and are therefore more likely to maintain motivation to take part in sport.

Dealing with young performers whose motives are only focused on obtaining external rewards is difficult. It is challenging to alter perspectives concerning sport and success already learnt by the child. For young performers motivated by external rewards, coaches should ideally be able to present practices so they provide additional motives and reasons for success.

## Examples of Drop-out Routes

### Route 1
The reward, which was the original motive, no longer has meaning to the young performer.

### Example
A 14-year-old girl goes to soccer practice because her parents praise her for doing so. But her parents praise her regardless of the effort she puts in or whether or not they thought she did well. This undermines the meaning of the praise and therefore does not motivate her any longer. Therefore, if seeking praise is the sole motive for participation, the performer may drop out.

### Route 2
When the reward ceases, the young performer has no apparent motive for further participation.

### Example
A 10-year-old boy wants to obtain a badge at his local swimming pool because he has seen his friends with one and he has seen them advertised on television. The badge motivates him to attend training and after a few weeks, he swims the required distance. As a result he is given the badge. Now that he has the badge, his main reason for swimming is no longer present and his participation wanes.

## Key strategies for enhancing young performers' motivation

- Present interesting practices which focus on improvement and effort.

- Vary practices and experiment with new and different ones – young performers tend to tire easily of the same task.

- Praise young performers for improvements and effort.
  NB  Praising them for poor effort or lack of improvement will undermine the value of the praise.

- Praise must not be confused with encouragement, which can be used to motivate performers.

- Praise must be consistent – all young performers should be praised regardless of ability and attitude if they satisfy the criteria (eg high effort, task-related improvement).

- Practices should focus on team/ group work with equal abilities and appropriately challenging tasks so young performers' needs for friendship, acceptance and competence are satisfied.

- Try to foster an environment which provides young performers with motives other than the gaining of extrinsic rewards. They should be encouraged to achieve task-related goals and not external rewards.

- Present tasks which focus on personal achievement as opposed to comparison with others.

## 3.4    Developing Independence

Ideally, coaches should aim to help young performers to make decisions for themselves. They need to feel independent (ie able to do things for themselves) and that they are the originator of their own actions. This will enhance their feelings of competence and achievement.

Young performers like to determine their own actions. If they do not feel in control of a situation (eg if they are told what to do all the time), then they might feel their success is due to other people's efforts rather than their own. Instead they prefer to be given the opportunity to do things for themselves. For example, if a young boy says 'Coach, I did it for myself', he is not saying he does not need the coach, rather that the coach has helped him do the task or performance for himself. The coach has therefore been instrumental in helping the boy to think and act independently. Coaches must strive to create environments which enable young performers to learn for themselves or at least feel they have some freedom of choice in practices or sessions.

As young performers mature they begin to identify the areas and activities which will satisfy their needs. Although people continue to find new areas in which to demonstrate competence as they move into adulthood, their scope becomes smaller due to constraints, work, family and other personal commitments. Children and young people, however, have not fully defined these areas and therefore have a greater scope to try different things. Young children up to seven years like to explore different games and skills for themselves. Therefore coaches should try to provide them with a variety of experiences which will enable them to try out different sports or activities. For example, in invasion games such as football, hockey or rugby, coaches may give all players in their group chances to play as an attacking, midfield or defending player. This gives them the

opportunity to see which position suits them best.

As competition is introduced (this can be as early as 6 or 7 years for children in some sports, but is more likely to be 10 to 12 years), success becomes more important. Consequently, children are likely to rely heavily on the coach to teach them how to become successful. Coaches should, however, encourage them to practise alone or with friends, away from the coaching session. This will help them to develop an independent approach which may become particularly important when training and practice time increases in late teens. When children are approximately 14 or over, coaches should further acknowledge the need for them to practise on their own and should give them some guidance on how to structure sessions and schedule their own practice. This progression is summarised in Table 6 on page 23.

Feelings of independence can be fostered by using practices which provide young performers with an investigative component (eg 'See if you can ... 'What happens if you ...' Have a go at ...'). Coaches often employ these types of examples and avoid using words like **must** and **should** which are associated with a controlling atmosphere and may reduce feelings of independence.

## 3.5    Effort and Ability

Young children have difficulty differentiating between ability and effort. They cannot tell the difference between someone who tries very hard at an activity and someone who has a natural or innate capacity to do the activity well. Therefore, in competitive situations, they do not know whether they have won because of superior ability or because they put in a lot of effort.

Children learn at about 10–12 years that some people are successful at an activity with little apparent application while others can only make a similar attainment by trying very hard. Their notions of effort and ability therefore become gradually more distinct and after the age of about 12, effort is seen to be the major factor under the child's control which can be changed. Usually, effort is seen as the main route to success with ability as a limiting factor. These developments can be seen in Table 6 on page 23.

Performers can view themselves as being highly **ego-oriented** or **task-oriented.** However, they are rarely either one or the other – most possess varying degrees of the qualities which represent both these orientations. A young performer who is mainly ego-oriented may not be able to differentiate between effort and ability very well, may not be able to recognise that ability is a limiting factor and therefore may have a tendency to blame their lack of success on not being good enough. These performers do not have motivational problems when they are winning, but when losing they find it difficult to apply themselves as they think their failure is because they lack ability. On the other hand, those who see that effort can be a measure of success are known as being task-oriented.

These two orientations are likely to influence the goals young performers pursue in sport. Task-oriented performers tend to do sports to enjoy and master the task, and are concerned only about the amount of effort they exert. Ego-oriented performers, however, tend to be concerned with how well they do and how good their ability is relative to others. Young performers who are interested in the task and put in a lot of effort, regardless of whether or not they want to win, are those likely to feel satisfied and persist in sport. Coaches should therefore foster task-orientation in their performers as much as possible. They should aim at least to create an environment which encourages them to focus on effort, rather than comparing themselves with others.

## 3.6 Creating an Effective Environment

The onus is on the coach to provide the best learning environment which will motivate young performers towards achieving their own goals. The practice environment is a great influence on whether a young performer adopts a predominantly ego or task achievement orientation (see Chapter 3.5). It can encourage young performers to achieve both outcome and process goals (see Chapter 3.2, page 25).

This environment can be adjusted according to the practices given (see Chapter 5.4), the language used by the coach (eg using words such as **effort** and **improvement** will create more of a task orientation than words such as **beating others**) and the type of feedback given (eg giving praise where it is due) can help to create a positive atmosphere.

Key strategies for enhancing a young performer's motivation are summarised by the mnemonic **TARGET**[1]:

sports coach UK

1    Adapted from Ames, C (1992).

**Task** – designing activities for individual challenge and active involvement.

Action points:

- During practice, give one or two technical instructions emphasising completion of the task to each performer or group.
- Provide a personal goal for each performer.
- Formulate practices which are varied and fun – this is not always easy to do but new and different ways of practising help young performers focus on the task and alleviate boredom.

**Authority** – involving athletes in decision-making and leadership roles as well as helping them develop self-management and self-monitoring skills.

Action points:

- Create practices in which performers could take turns in being the lead performer (eg the server/scorer in a tennis practice or an evaluator in a football practice).
- Provide performers with practices that encourage them to discover answers for themselves.

**Recognition** – acknowledging and recognising individual progress and improvement.

Action points:

- Avoid sessions which focus solely on performers comparing themselves with others – try to create challenges in which performers are trying to improve their own personal standards (ie where they compare their performance to their own standards and not the performance of others).

**Grouping** – using flexible group arrangements so young performers can learn from each other.

Action points:

- Give performers the opportunity to work together to solve problems or master a task within the activity – eg ask the group: 'See if you can find out how to kick the ball to give it height or make it move along the ground'.

- Try to match the abilities of performers when they are playing competitive games – if they win or lose too easily, they are more likely to lose interest or confidence respectively.
  NB  If this is not possible, set performers personal goals within the game which are unrelated to the score.

**Evaluation** – assessing young performers in terms of individual progress, improvement and mastery.

Action points:

- Give performers feedback and encouragement if they reach the agreed goals, especially those which are based on personal improvement within the task.

**Time** – providing opportunities and time for improvements and goals to be attained.

Action points:

- Organise a proper schedule or timetable for the agreed goals to be achieved – monitor progress to identify any changes in performance or if any goals need to be amended.

## 3.7    Friendship and Acceptance

While children gain satisfaction from their independent actions, they also like to feel they belong to a valued group. As they reach late childhood and early adolescence (about 12–14 years), being part of a close-knit group of friends becomes more important. Sport gives them the opportunity to be with their friends (social continuation) or make new friends (social growth).

The coach must be aware that for some young performers, friendship may be the sole motive for participation (ie some performers may only be interested in the activity because their friends are participating). Coaches should try to ensure that in these cases, the performers' needs are satisfied not by separating them unnecessarily in group work, but by presenting other goals which offer some challenge and intrinsic reward.

Although friendships can sometimes have a negative effect on learning, particularly if one person is disruptive to the rest of the group, they can also facilitate learning. Coaches should be aware of the friendships developing in their team, group or squad and use these as the basis for smaller group work. Young performers may feel more comfortable having a friend alongside them, particularly in new situations or practices. However, in other situations, it may sometimes be better to mix the groups so that young performers have the opportunity to practise with new peers. This can relieve boredom and encourage social growth.

Key strategies to help young performers relate to each other within sessions:

- Be aware of the friendships between performers in the group.

- Encourage group work so young performers can be with their friends but also mix with others.

- Understand that young performers like to talk with their friends – make them aware of the possible disruption this causes during sessions and inform them there will be an opportunity to talk to each other during breaks or after the session.

- Allow frequent breaks in practice, particularly for young children – this will give them an opportunity to talk to each other.

Coaches should be aware that peer influences outside training or practice can negatively affect commitment.

As children move into adolescence they become more socially active and peer groups become increasingly important and influential. For instance, a performer who may be committed as a child may become less committed because values change and the relative importance of sport decreases.

The coach should not force performers to attend training and practice. This may lead to performers training because they feel they should rather than because they want to. Ultimately they may rebel against training and drop out from the sport completely. Coaches should help young performers attain a balance between their sport and social life. They should acknowledge peer and friendship commitments but also help young performers value their sport as an integral part of their lives.

## 3.8 Self-esteem

If young performers feel they are good at a task (ie they can achieve its outcome and can do it for themselves), it is likely to increase their self-esteem. Often self-esteem in sport is an outcome or by-product of competent practice. Coaches should therefore try to ensure young performers have successive experiences of achievement so they feel good about the sport or activity.

Having a high self-esteem in sport has many positive effects on young performers (eg it can encourage them to work harder, enjoy training and competition). However, it can also be very fragile. A bad experience, such as being shown to be incompetent at a sports task, particularly in front of friends, or losing to a lower ranked performer, may result in lowered self-esteem which could discourage further participation. This is particularly true for teenagers who are very self-conscious, have mood swings and are under pressure from other factors such as school work and peer groups. Coaches should avoid giving critical feedback or disciplining young performers in front of others, particularly their peers.

Coaches can help to foster and maintain self-esteem in sport by providing sessions which will help young performers feel they are achieving their goals. In the competitive sphere, they can also provide alternatives which will help guard against self-esteem in sport being adversely affected by defeat or losing. For example, a team might lose a basketball game but the coach can guide players into thinking about the reasons for the loss and focus on positive aspects of the performance.

The coach might say 'OK team – you lost the game today, but remember the turns I told you to do in practice? You did them very well'. This way they can protect feelings of competence and emphasise good, task-related points. Chapter 3.2 (page 25) explains about the benefits of using process goals – these will also help to protect the self-esteem in sport of young performers.

## 3.9 Enjoyment

Enjoyment is a key aspect of intrinsic motivation (Chapter 3.3, page 26). Coaches should recognise the inherent pleasure that some activities bring to young performers and sometimes structure practices which enable them to have more freedom to practise the aspects they like best. This opportunity can help develop their independence as well as giving them pleasure. It may also help to alleviate the intensity or repetition of some sessions.

For some sports performers, enjoyment may not be the only reason for engaging in sport. There are often other motives such as the need for competence, achievement and independence. These motives may help young performers to engage in practices which they may not necessarily enjoy.

*Coaches should aim to plan sessions which are enjoyable and productive.*

Key strategies for coaches to help plan enjoyable sessions:

- Vary practices.
- Provide breaks from intense or repetitive tasks by offering opportunities to practise more enjoyable tasks which have some element of choice (eg 'OK, take ten minutes to practise your favourite shot with your partner').
- Provide a rationale for doing hard, difficult or challenging training and make sure the emphasis is on enjoyment for the times in between.
- Empathise with young performers – acknowledge that they might not enjoy some of the training but reinforce the benefits they will gain.

## 3.10   Rules and Fair Play

Rules can teach valuable lessons about sport and fair play. It is often useful to minimise rules for younger children as they can be too complex for them to cope with. Coaches should aim to keep practices and games simple for young children and gradually encourage them to discover why sports have certain rules. For example, the badminton underarm serve rule need not be taught to beginners and could be introduced later on as a guided discovery exercise (the coach might ask: 'How could you prevent the game being dominated by serve?'). For more information on modifying sports, refer to Chapter 5.5.

The coach has a responsibility to teach young performers values in sport and why fair play is at the core of the sporting ethos. Some performers may be more inclined to lie or cheat in competition. Coaches should condemn such behaviour and emphasise that they are unacceptable in sport. Young performers need to know why there are rules and why it is not in the spirit of fair play to cheat. In addition, it should be made clear to them that if they are ever going to play to a high standard, they will never be allowed to cheat as the games will have referees or umpires to make the decisions. Coaches should lead by example and promote fair play. In doing so, they should enforce fair play rules in practice to ensure children are used to, and aware of, such regulations when it comes to competition.

---

### TASK

Think of the basic rules of your sport. Are there any changes that could be made to make it more suitable for children?

Think how you would design a practice competition for some young (10–12 year old), beginner performers which has modified rules to maximise enjoyment and minimise complicated explanations.

For instance if you were modifying rugby, you would pay particular attention to ensure children were safe (by introducing a rule of no tackling) and they all had a good chance of receiving the ball. Consider also the questions you might ask the children to get them to think about additional rules. Remember your aim is to try to make them tell you the rules you omitted.

## 3.11 Young Performers and Competition

Some believe that competition encourages too much focus on winning rather than on the quality of the performance (ie achieving a goal will create winners and losers). For example, coaches, parents and teachers can all be guilty of attaching too much importance to the result of a competition rather than to the other benefits it can provide.

However, competition plays a vital role in the development of young performers and its merits are sometimes understated. Experience of competitive situations can help performers to improve important tactical, technical and decision-making skills within a realistic environment.

That said, competition is not an effective method of improving young performers' all-round skills and should therefore take second place to a well structured, systematic training programme that provides a more effective means of developing their individual and team skills.

Coaches should encourage young performers to view competition as:

- an opportunity to try out all the movements and skills they work on in training
- a test of personal skill
- an enjoyable experience
- a learning experience regardless of the actual outcome.

Competitive structures (such as rankings, scoring systems or individual/team games) vary between different sporting activities. It is important that coaches are aware of these structures and provide young performers with the appropriate opportunities for competitive endeavours (if this matches the mutually agreed goals). Most importantly, they must be on hand to help and advise young performers in making decisions about the competitions they have agreed to enter or work towards.

Competition must not be seen as the be all and end all – this will result in excessive value being attached to the competition outcome, which, if not a victory, could be detrimental to motivation and future participation.

Coaches should help young performers to recognise there are still lessons to be learnt from a competition where the outcome is not a victory. The performers will be motivated to participate further if they feel they have gained something from the experience, particularly if it is task-related. For example, a coach might say 'You did not win the game today because you did not use the shot you did in practice – with a little more practice, you may be able to use it next time'. This provides the performer with some task-related instruction. While it contains some criticism, it is constructive criticism. In this example, the performer is encouraged to practise the desired shot so the performance is better next time. This emphasises the importance of using process goals (Chapter 3.2, page 25).

Young performers, who can have very fragile self-esteem and self-regard particularly in front of their parents and peers, can be adversely affected by losing. On such occasions, coaches should not just be a source of comfort but rather help young performers to draw out positive aspects from a performance (eg identify areas to work on so they perform better in the next game, or parts of their performance that were much better than in the previous game). In addition, coaches can help young performers identify reasons for losing which may not be under the performers' control (eg their opponent played very well), can be changed in the future and are not related to their lack of competence. This can have a more positive effect on their self-esteem.

Winning can also be an important aspect of a young performer's learning process. However, coaches should try to ensure that it is not the sole criteria for success. Instead, it may be appropriate to outline to young performers reasons why they won and what aspects they did well to attain the success. Too much focus on the outcome may result in them measuring success purely on whether they won or lost. This may make them insensitive to other measures of success such as effort and personal improvement.

## 3.12    Summary

Young performers have a number of different motives for taking part in sport. Coaches should recognise these motives and how they are likely to change with developmental and training age. Sessions should be planned and designed to help performers achieve their goals. They should be enjoyable as well as productive.

Competition plays a vital role in the development of young performers, but it must be managed properly within a well structured training programme.

# CHAPTER FOUR:
# Physical Development

Children are growing and developing throughout childhood and adolescence. Coaches need to be aware of the physical changes taking place as these will affect the practices that young performers should be advised to do. Physical development will also dictate the frequency, intensity, duration and type of training that coaches plan.

By the end of this chapter, you should be able to:

- identify the key aspects of physical development

- explain the implications of physical development for practices, training sessions and programmes for your young performers.

## 4.0    Growth Trends

People grow from birth until they reach their peak height at about 20 years of age. However, the rate of growth is not consistent. Generally, children experience two rapid periods of growth, one during infancy (first two years of life) and a second **adolescent growth spurt** which occurs during puberty. Between these periods of rapid growth, a slower, more consistent rate of growth takes place. There are few gender differences in terms of height until puberty, after which boys appear significantly taller. Girls usually experience the adolescent growth spurt slightly earlier than boys.

actionplus

Of specific relevance to the coach are the relative proportions of the body during these phases of growth, particularly the adolescent growth spurt. A coach should know that before puberty children tend to have disproportionately longer arms and legs in relation to their body. Young performers may appear to be all arms and legs at this stage, and this may affect their ability to control their movements.

Coaches need to appreciate that any apparent clumsiness is usually the result of their developmental stage rather than deficiencies in their ability.

### TASK

How would you respond to young performers who are experiencing difficulties in their motor control due to their changing body proportions?

Compare your thoughts with the strategies listed below.

Possible considerations include:

- taking into account growth stages when teaching new movements

- recognising limitations and not expecting too much

- helping young performers understand changes and reassuring them that they will soon adapt to these

- grouping young performers of the same developmental stage together.

## 4.1    The Adolescent Growth Spurt

The adolescent pubertal growth spurt is a period of rapid physical, psychological and social change. At this stage, children and young people experience rapid increases in height and weight which result in changing body proportions. Consequently, movements which have been mastered may appear to become less coordinated as the child struggles to cope with heavier but substantially stronger limbs and a larger body. As the graphs on page 43 show (Figures 2 and 3), girls tend to experience these changes up to two years before boys – in early adolescence, they often appear physically more mature and taller than boys. At the same time there is a large inter-individual variation in the rates of growth so that at any given age, some children and young people may seem taller and more developed than others. It is therefore important that the coach recognises the developmental age rather than just the chronological age of young performers when planning practices and sessions.

Figures 2 and 3 on page 43 show trends in growth for males and females.

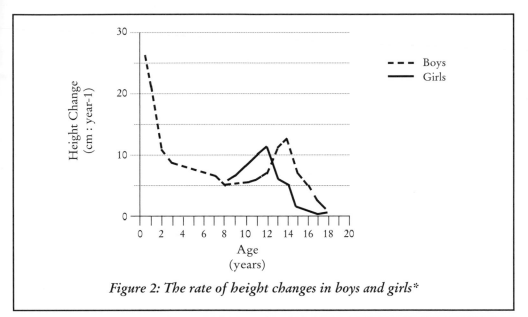

*Figure 2: The rate of height changes in boys and girls\**

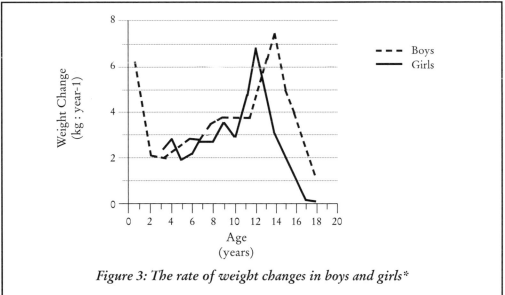

*Figure 3: The rate of weight changes in boys and girls\**

\*   Adapted from Wilmore, JH and Costill, DL (1994) **Physiology of sport and exercise.**
Champaign IL, Human Kinetics, p403.

---

**TASK**

Consider the changes you might make to your practices to cater for young performers of different developmental ages.

Compare your thoughts with the strategies listed below.

---

In adapting sessions to cater for young performers at different stages of growth, coaches should:

- separate performers into groups according to developmental ages – this is particularly important in contact sports
- try to tailor the positions or location of the performers according to body size where separation into groups is not possible (eg in netball, avoid pairing a small goal shooter with a tall goalkeeper).

## 4.2    Skeletal Development

The skeleton supports soft tissues in the body such as the skeletal muscles and protects others such as the brain, heart and lungs.

It has three main functions:

- support
- protection
- transmission of force.

In children the skeleton has to allow for growth. It cannot therefore be fully ossified[1] and as a result, bones are softer and less rigid than those of adults as they are still developing. At key points in the major bones, there are softer parts where new bone is deposited to allow growth to occur. These points are known as epiphyseal or **growth plates.** The majority of bone growth occurs at these plates. As the bone lengthens, the new bone or cartilage slowly hardens and becomes ossified. The full ossification of the bones is not complete until about twenty years of age.

---

1    Ossification is the development process of the skeleton.

Therefore bones, and in particular the growth plates, may become damaged if subjected to excessive force.

In addition, the attachments of muscle to bone (tendons) and bone to bone (ligaments) are also developing as children grow. The sites where muscle is attached to bone are often soft and weak during development and so if excessive load or force is placed upon them, bone or tendon damage is likely to occur. This could be sudden (acute) damage such as a fracture or torn tendon caused by excessive force, or repetitive (chronic) damage such as a hairline/stress fracture caused by continual overload.

The following list shows examples of activities which may place excessive force on joints and bones and as a result may cause bone, tendon or ligament damage. Dangerous activities include:

- bounding or jumping on hard surfaces (eg plyometric[1] training on tarmac or concrete)

- vigorous throwing or catching with heavy objects

- playing with rackets, bats or other implements that are too heavy

- lifting weights that are too heavy

- continued rapid changes of direction and acceleration on hard surfaces.

To minimise skeletal and tendon damage, coaches should:

- avoid practices on hard surfaces – use tartan[2] or grass if possible

- make sure equipment is suitable for the developmental stage of the child

- encourage young performers to develop strength using exercises which involve supporting their own body weight

- not introduce weight training too soon – start with very light weights with high repetitions and progress slowly

- avoid practices involving very high impact (eg plyometric training, bounding, power jumping) until late adolescence.

1   Plyometric training is an advanced method of developing power.

2   A type of synthetic running or playing surface.

## 4.3 Responses to Exercise

Most sports require a certain degree of fitness. Fitness is a general term which encompasses all the necessary physical adaptations important to function in a sporting activity (eg speed, strength, endurance, flexibility). Clearly there are different types of fitness. For instance, the type required for a sprint swimmer or runner (eg speed) is different from that of a longer distance swimmer or runner (eg endurance). In games such as football and hockey, however, it is desirable to have both fast pace and endurance to maintain repeated short bursts of speed.

Young performers as well as adults require fitness in order to cope with the demands of training and competition. Their fitness, however, must be appropriate for their particular sport or activity. They can use similar types of training to adults but the frequency, volume and intensity of the training will need to be adapted to suit their stage of development[1].

## Short-term cardiovascular effects

Prolonged, sub-maximal activities such as long-distance running, cycling and swimming will put considerable stress on the muscles, heart and lungs. The muscles have an increased demand for energy which is supplied by carbohydrate and fat sources located inside the muscle and liver cells. Oxygen is required for this energy to be released and this is supplied by the blood. The blood receives oxygen from the lungs and is pumped to the muscles and other organs of the body by the heart. This entire system of uptake and supply is known as the **cardiovascular system**. As the rate of activity (eg running speed) increases so does the demand for energy. Consequently, the heart beats faster and the rate of breathing rises to meet this demand. These are the short-term effects of exercise and activity. Children are particularly suited to these low-level aerobic activities and cope well with increased cardiovascular demands, provided they are sub-maximal.

1   For more information, you are recommended to attend the **scUK** workshop *Fitness and Training* and read its accompanying resource *Physiology and Performance* (complimentary with the workshop). All **scUK** resources are available from **Coachwise 1st4sport** (tel 0113-201 5555 or visit www.1st4sport.com).

2   For a more detailed explanation, you are recommended to read the **scUK** resource *An Introduction to Sports Physiology*. All **scUK** resources are available from **Coachwise 1st4sport** (tel 0113-201 5555 or visit www.1st4sport.com).

Young performers are often quite active and seldom need to reverse the effects of years of inactivity unlike many adults.

## Long-term cardiovascular effects

Over a period of time, repeated bouts of prolonged activity with recovery periods result in the muscles, heart and lungs becoming more efficient at supplying and meeting the demand for energy in exercise[2]. In children these adaptations occur in the same way as they do in adults (ie they become better able to cope with prolonged activity). It is therefore important that young performers do some endurance training in order to increase their fitness level for their sport. This may be relevant to most sports from endurance activities to games where running and jogging is interspersed with sprinting (eg football, rugby and hockey). Court games such as tennis and squash also require endurance training to enable young performers to train effectively and recover quickly from the short energy bursts.

## Speed and anaerobic effects

An anaerobic system uses muscle carbohydrate stores without the use of oxygen to provide the energy for short, high-intensity activity. This is a rapid process but has the side effect of releasing waste products like lactic acid which can interfere with muscle function and cause premature fatigue. In games and sprint sports, the anaerobic system is the major source of energy, and training can improve speed and recovery rates. Children do not cope well with short bursts of very high-intensity activity or repeated short recovery sprint work. However, as they develop, so does their capacity for anaerobic work.

Coaches should be aware of these limitations and use anaerobic work sparingly with performers of a young developmental and training age. At this stage, training should focus on technique and endurance work, with anaerobic work being introduced gradually and progressively as they develop. In preparation for competition, young performers should still not do too much anaerobic training and should rely on their aerobic fitness. Table 7 on page 48 gives coaches guidelines for the types of conditioning work young performers should be doing at different stages of development. The guidelines, however, will be subject to the type of sport involved and should be adapted according to developmental rather than chronological age.

*Table 7: Guidelines for types of conditioning work*

| Age Group | Anaerobic/Sprint Training | Aerobic/Endurance Training | Mixed or Multi-sprint Type Training |
|---|---|---|---|
| Young children | Keep to a minimum | Most training should be low-level aerobic, focus on correct technique | Keep limited, only in games situations – keep a high focus on playing skills |
| Pre-adolescents | Introduce 1–2 sessions per week, long recovery intervals | Higher level aerobic training possible, prolonged intervals[1], long recovery | Introduce gradually into training, again no more than 1–2 sessions of prolonged multi-sprint work, focus on maintaining playing skills within pace work (eg practice matches of up to ten minutes) |
| Early adolescents | Increase to up to three sessions per week, long recovery | Highest aerobic level (ie just below maximum speed), prolonged intervals, long recovery | As above, progression to up to three sessions per week, keep practice match times down to 10–15 minutes per half |
| Late adolescents | Up to four sessions per week, recovery interval can be shortened | High-level, longer intervals, shortened recovery | Up to four sessions per week, increase practice match times to 20–30 minutes per half |
| Post-adolescents | Full anaerobic training possible, short recovery intervals | Prolonged high-level training possible, intervals not necessary | Full match times possible in training, but still keep number of sessions to minimum due to the stressful nature of such work |

1   Prolonged intervals should enable young performers to recover between activities.

## 4.4　Strength

Strength is the ability of the muscles to apply force. As children develop physically so does the size and therefore the strength of their muscles. There is likely to be a wide range in the size and strength of the muscles between young performers of different chronological, developmental and training ages, particularly around puberty. Strength continues to increase until the end of adolescence and therefore a young child cannot be expected to execute strength activities in the same way as more mature children and adults. Coaches should make sure the type and conditions of strength training are suitable for the developmental and training age of young performers as well as their chronological age.

There are different types of strength which can be classified on a continuum from **absolute strength** at one end to **strength endurance** at the other.

Absolute (or muscular) strength can be viewed as the maximum force applied by the muscle while strength endurance is the capacity of the muscles to sustain or repeat contractions without fatigue. As different sports require different types of strength, training needs to vary according to the demands of the sport, as well as the developmental and training age of young performers.

Strength can be improved by resistance training which can occur in many forms (eg body weight exercises, partner-assisted resistance exercises, free-weight and fixed-weight resistance training, and elastic cord training). Each can be effective for different activities. Coaches should know the strength demands of their sport and be able to advise young performers on the exercises that are most suitable for them[1].

Coaches should not recommend that young children (under ten years) participate in excessive and specific load-bearing resistance training.

---

1　For more information on improving all aspects of fitness, including strength, you are recommended to attend the **scUK** workshop *Fitness and Training* and read its accompanying resource *Physiology and Performance* (complimentary with the workshop). All **scUK** resources are available from **Coachwise 1st4sport** (tel 0113-201 5555 or visit www.1st4sport.com).

Instead, they should encourage them to engage in exercises which:

- involve using their own body weight (eg press-ups, sit-ups)

- can be modified according to training level (eg box press-up progressing to half-box and then full press-up – see Figure 4)

- are located towards the endurance end of the continuum.

For young performers, resistance exercises using their own body weight can be incorporated into a varied cardiovascular training circuit. As well as general strength exercises (eg press-ups, sit-ups), circuit training (as it is more commonly referred to) may also include exercises that are specific to the sport. For example, a tennis player may simulate the action and recovery of an overhead by moving backwards, leaping upwards and moving quickly forwards again. Young performers are far more likely to enjoy and benefit from this type of varied training, than from rigorous weight training that is non-sport-specific and which may cause injury.

Contrary to previous beliefs, pre-pubescent children (approximately 10–12 years) can benefit from carefully supervised resistance training which is geared towards the endurance end of

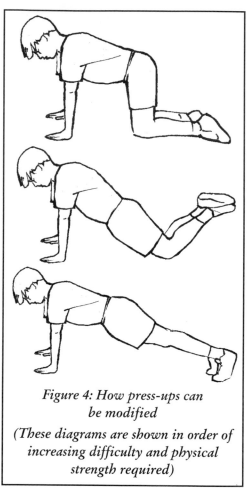

*Figure 4: How press-ups can be modified*

*(These diagrams are shown in order of increasing difficulty and physical strength required)*

the strength training continuum (ie high repetition, low resistance). This training can be done using their own body weight, or light free or fixed (machine) weights (the weight machines must be adjustable enough to suit the smaller body proportions of young children).

All sessions must be carefully supervised by a qualified fitness instructor and the progression needs to be gentle and gradual to prevent muscle, tendon or ligament damage, and the development of poor technique.

For post-adolescent performers, coaches may, in some cases, encourage them to do power or plyometric type training on appropriate surfaces (eg bounding or power skipping on a tartan or grass surface). However, a good base of strength is advised before any training of this type is introduced. It is important that exercises are used sparingly and introduced gradually – if not, this type of training can cause injury.

At this stage of development, coaches can also encourage performers to progress to slightly heavier weights which are geared more towards the absolute strength end of the continuum. This should be a gradual process. As performers progress they will eventually be able to use strength exercises which encompass the full range of the absolute strength/strength endurance continuum. Table 8 on page 52 shows the recommended strength training guidelines for performers at various stages of development.

Another factor which will affect the strength training of young performers is the amount of time allocated to training and practice sessions. While strength training may be a prerequisite for success in some sports, it is usually used in conjunction with the specific training for that sport. Strength training should therefore be done in addition to, rather than in place of, specific training for the sport.

*Table 8: Guidelines for strength training for young performers*

| Stage of Development | Types of Training | Repetitions | Times Per Week | Continuum | Comments |
|---|---|---|---|---|---|
| Young children | Own body weight (eg press-ups, sit-ups) | High no of reps, low weight | Up to two | Endurance | To be used as part of general cardiovascular circuit |
| Pre-adolescents | Own body weight | High no of reps, low weight | Up to two | Endurance, some strength | Some specific sessions but mainly part of circuit |
| Early adolescents | Own body weight, some specific resistance (eg elastic cords, light dumb-bells) | High to moderate no of reps, small to medium weight | Up to two | Endurance, some mid-range strength | Introduce more specific resistance exercises slowly, 1–2 sessions on resistance training per week plus 1–2 circuits |
| Late adolescents | Some body weight, free and fixed weights (eg weights machines) | Moderate to low no of reps, medium to high weight | Up to three | Mix of endurance, mid-range strength and some end-range strength | Can be all specific sessions provided cardiovascular training is met elsewhere |
| Post-adolescents | Full range of modes plus plyometrics | Full range including power exercises | Up to four | Full range, sport-specific | Power training introduced but on low-impact surfaces and used sparingly |

## 4.5  Flexibility

Flexibility is the range of movement in the joints and will affect the success of performers in many sports. Any limitations in flexibility may compromise some sport-specific movements. However, flexibility training will increase the range of movement and therefore needs to be built into the training programme for many young performers.

Children (particularly girls) tend to be very flexible. As they become older, however, children (particularly boys) may lose some of their flexibility. People tend to lose flexibility progressively throughout their adult life, and it is therefore important from a performance and health point of view to help young performers develop and maintain their flexibility. As young performers tend to be very flexible in the first place, they should not engage in intensive, ballistic (bouncing), partner-assisted or gravity-assisted stretching. This could result in damage to the muscle attachments to the growth plates (eg Osgood-Schlatter's disease). Instead gentle, progressive, passive stretching exercises are recommended where young performers hold the stretch when they feel slight discomfort for approximately 10–20 seconds. They should not stretch beyond this point and never attempt to stretch when they are cold. Coaches should emphasise the importance of normal breathing when stretching – people are often tempted to hold their breath during the stretch and this can restrict movement.

Coaches should encourage young performers to stretch as part of their warm-up before sessions. They should demonstrate how to stretch, emphasise correct and safe techniques, check young performers are stretching correctly, and ensure the stretching is preceded by some cardiovascular work (eg jogging, gentle movement exercises). When the purpose of stretching is to warm up as opposed to extend the range of movement, stretch positions do not have to be held for very long (approximately ten seconds). The purpose of stretching as part of the warm-up is not really to improve flexibility – the main aim is to help young performers:

- prepare for the physical demands of their sport

- learn how to stretch and why it is important before training and competition

- protect themselves against injury during the sessions

- maintain their current levels of flexibility

- adopt safe and healthy habits
- improve their performance
- highlight any particular weakness that may need extra attention.

Young performers should also be encouraged to do some gentle stretching after training sessions or competitions (as part of the cool-down). This will help to prevent the onset of stiffness in the muscles.

## 4.6 Safety Considerations

There are many factors which can affect young performers' response to exercise. To ensure young performers are safe when they take part in sport, coaches need to consider the effects of:

- temperature control
- injury
- illness
- other factors.

### Temperature control

Young performers are less able than adults to cope with great temperature extremes. Since their bodies are smaller, the surface area of their skin in relation to their total body volume is much greater than that of adults.

This makes them more efficient heat exchangers. In hot environments children can gain heat very quickly but if their core temperature rises too much it can lead to overheating or **hyperthermia.** This could result in a number of serious conditions such as dehydration, heat exhaustion or heat stroke, which must be treated immediately. Hyperthermia can happen very quickly when young performers are engaged in high-intensity training and competition, and the coach should therefore look out for signs of overheating (see Table 9 on page 55).

Conversely, in cold environments children can lose heat very quickly. In addition to their large surface area, they tend to have a low amount of body fat which may exacerbate heat loss in the cold. Too great a loss of body heat can lead to **hypothermia** which can again be very serious. Hypothermia is a fall in core temperature which could cause abnormal or irregular heartbeats. It is therefore important for coaches to detect quickly any signs of cold stress in young performers (see Table 9 on page 55).

*Table 9: Signs of heat stress and cold stress*

| Signs of Heat Stress | Signs of Cold Stress |
|---|---|
| • Cramp<br>• Cold clammy skin<br>• Reduced or profuse sweating<br>• Lack of coordination<br>• Extreme fatigue and fainting<br>• Flushed appearance<br>• Dizziness and disorientation | • Shivering<br>• Pale complexion<br>• Inability to talk clearly<br>• Limited movements |

## TASK

Think of the precautions you would take on a very cold day and a very hot day to prevent problems of thermoregulation with the young performers you coach.

Compare your ideas with Table 10.

*Table 10: Precautions on a very hot day and a very cold day*

| Precautions on a Very Hot Day | Precautions on a Very Cold Day |
|---|---|
| • Have water on hand and encourage young performers to drink before, during and after training<br>• Be aware of signs of undue distress and lack of enjoyment<br>• Ensure young performers wear clothing designed to cool the body<br>• Organise regular breaks | • Make sure young performers wear the appropriate cold weather clothing<br>• Try to minimise exposure to cold<br>• Ensure young performers are adequately warmed up<br>• Try to minimise breaks where young performers are doing little activity<br>• Make sure young performers move to an indoor location as soon as possible after the practice session |

General points to consider:

- Tell young performers to listen to their bodies and tell you if they are too tired, hot or cold.

- Write down on a handout or tell parents what equipment or clothing their children will need to bring for the sessions.

- React early to any signs of distress.

- Ensure you wear appropriate clothing and practise what you preach – be a good role model.

## Injury

Injuries are a frequent occurrence in sport. However, coaches can help to minimise the risk of injury by advising performers on how to stay fit and prepare for training and competition. Young performers are often less capable than adults in recognising their limitations or the consequences of their actions which may cause injury to others. They therefore rely on their coach to educate them on the dangers of certain actions and how they can prevent injury to themselves and others.

NB  Many of these can be sport-specific, so make sure you are up to date on all the latest safety precautions of your sport – your governing body should have guidelines.

Coaches should take young performers through an adequate warm-up procedure prior to training, and cool-down post-training, to minimise the risk of injury due to cold muscles or joints (eg muscle tears or joint sprains). In addition, they should be encouraged to warm up, cool down and follow safe practice at all times (eg at practice sessions on their own, at competitions, playing other sports)[1].

## Illness

Sometimes young performers are affected by illness, particularly during the winter months. However minor the illness (eg a common cold or influenza), it should not be ignored as it could have potential side effects. For instance, training with an infection or virus may create excessive stress on a child's or young person's body, particularly the heart. Coaches should make sure young performers are aware of the hazards associated with training

For more information on injuries, you are recommended to attend both the **scUK** workshop *Injury Prevention and Management* and the British Red Cross/**scUK** workshop *Emergency First Aid for Sport*. Both have an accompanying resource. All **scUK** resources are available ɔm **Coachwise 1st4sport** (tel 0113-201 5555 or visit www.1st4sport.com).

when ill and should always encourage them to rest until they have recovered. In addition, coaches should know of any special conditions that may be exacerbated by exercise or present a possible health problem (eg asthma, diabetes). They should have access to, or ensure the performer brings to the sessions, any preventative medication (eg inhaler for asthma sufferers). If unsure, coaches should check with parents what action to take if a child suffers with a specific condition during the session.

## Other factors

The onus is on coaches to ensure that during their sessions, the equipment and play area is safe. All equipment must be checked prior to, during and after training sessions to prevent any potential hazards. Young performers can be very headstrong and may leap with great enthusiasm into a task before thinking about the possible consequences. Coaches must therefore warn them of dangers when using sport-specific equipment and play areas. Young performers, particularly those who are new to the sport, should be guided through a specific safety routine prior to any practice and more experienced performers should be encouraged to set a good example.

Such routines are clearly vital in sports such as javelin or archery when the risk of injury is very serious if no routine is in operation.

Weather conditions may also be a safety hazard. For instance on a wet day, outdoor surfaces may be very slippery so it is important to advise performers on how these conditions might affect their form and how they can take extra care.

Most sports have been developed for adults. This means the dimensions of the play areas, the equipment and the rules are all tailored to accommodate adults' capabilities. However, the physical demands of adult sport are often too much for young performers. Their physical immaturity may prevent them from fulfilling the aims of the sport but more importantly may result in injury. For instance, adult equipment (eg cricket bats, tennis rackets) is often too heavy for children and the play areas/pitches may be too large. Modifying or adapting sports to suit physical stages of development means that young performers can be safer, are more able to gain a sense of achievement and are more likely to enjoy the sport. Chapter 5.5 explains in greater detail the benefits and principles of modifying sports.

## Key strategies in injury prevention and ensuring safe practice or training sessions

Coaches should:

- inform young performers of the potential dangers and risk of injury to themselves and others from certain actions, movements and equipment

- listen to young performers

- look for signs of stress, distress and lack of enjoyment

- know what to do in the event of injury (eg location of first aid kit, qualified first aider, telephone)

- stress the necessity of appropriate safety equipment for the activity (eg shin pads for football, mouthguards for rugby)

- tell young performers to stop when they feel very uncomfortable or in pain

- modify sports to suit the physical capabilities of young performers.

## 4.7    Summary

Coaches should know the physical changes that young performers go through while developing. They should recognise that performers of a given chronological age will vary physically according to their developmental age. Young performers are continually developing in terms of their height, body size, limb proportions, cardiovascular endurance, anaerobic capacity and strength. Coaches must look out for these changes and know how to cater for them. It is important for coaches to balance the physical training of young performers – it needs to be appropriate to the sport but also to the developmental stage of the child. In addition, coaches should be aware of any problems which could arise during practices, such as hyperthermia and hypothermia. They must acknowledge and take appropriate steps to minimise the additional risks that illness and injury pose to young performers doing sport. Coaches should know how to modify sports and games to suit the physical capabilities of performers.

# CHAPTER FIVE:
# Skill Development

Skill is related to why, when and how movements are executed. Young performers can experience tremendous improvements in skill as they develop and this can be enhanced through careful planning and guidance by the coach. It is therefore particularly rewarding for coaches to help young performers in their endeavours to improve skill.

By the end of this chapter, you should be able to:

- plan coaching practices, sessions and programmes to maximise learning and enjoyment

- adapt your coaching according to the skill level of the child.

## 5.0　　Basic Movement Patterns

From birth, children begin to explore the range of possibilities for movement. Some of these movements are reflexive, such as the righting reflex in which newborns react to sudden movements by the opposite movement of the head. Slowly this type of reflex is suppressed and by the age of about two years is replaced by more complex, refined movements (eg reaching and grasping).

Children learn to reach out for an object and grasp it by trial and error. Early on they will grasp but not reach or vice versa. However, given the appropriate opportunity for experience, they slowly learn to coordinate these two actions. This is the beginning of the child learning basic movement patterns of the limbs and body. Young children learn these movements more quickly if they are given the appropriate stimuli and opportunity to try movements out for themselves (eg bright coloured objects and encouragement from parents). Most people learn movements by *having a go* and this concept is relevant to all ages, not only young children.

actionplus

Basic movement patterns include static balance (eg standing on one leg), dynamic balance (eg landing on one leg), locomotion (eg crawling and walking) and manipulation (eg reaching and grasping). Children should be encouraged to learn basic movement patterns early on as they serve as a precursor for more complex movements which are developed at a later stage. It is difficult to learn more complex movements unless these basic patterns have been fully developed.

## 5.1 Fundamental Movement Patterns

Once children have learnt basic movement patterns (usually this is up to the ages of six and seven), they begin to develop more complex movements. These involve the basic movements (balance, stability, locomotion and manipulation) but in an ordered, purposeful manner (see Table 11). Developing fundamental movement patterns is important as they will help children to learn sport-specific movements. Until these have been learnt, children will find it difficult to coordinate movements in the changing environment of a game, sport or competition.

*Table 11: Examples of specific movement (with increasing complexity) in the fundamental movement skill categories*
*(Adapted from Gallahue and Osman, 1992)*

| Movement Category | Example of Movement | Description |
|---|---|---|
| Dynamic balance | Running | Child learns to balance while moving at speed |
|  | Beam balance | Child learns to balance on narrow beam while moving forwards |
| Static balance | Single foot balance | Child learns to balance on one foot unaided for 3–5 seconds |
| Locomotion | Standing long jump | Child learns to coordinate upper and lower body muscles in ordered fashion to get maximum distance from a standing start |
| Manipulation | Striking tennis ball with racket | Child learns to find appropriate ball position, body position and racket position to make contact and hit ball |

## 5.2 Stages of Learning

Coaches should recognise that young performers go through three different phases in the acquisition of fundamental movement patterns; these are often referred to as stages of learning – **stage 1** (cognitive phase), **stage 2** (associative phase) and **stage 3** (autonomous phase).

During the first stage of learning, young performers are beginning to grasp the way their muscles and limbs must move to complete an action. They have to think carefully about what they should do and this means their movements are usually jerky, slow and not very fluid. This is because they have to think about what to do and the translation of this into the action takes time. Coaches can help this process by encouraging young performers to focus on external cues relating to the outcome of the movement rather than the movement itself. An example of this might be asking performers to say aloud *bounce* when a tennis or squash ball hits the ground and *hit* when their racket strikes the ball. While this reminds them of the purpose of the task, it does not interfere with their feel of the movement. Young performers rely heavily on feedback from the coach at this stage of learning. This feedback, however,

should be restricted to the most important or general aspects of the movement as the performers do not yet have a clear picture of the action.

At the second stage of learning, young performers have to think less about the movement. This is because some parts of the movement have been committed to memory and are more consistent. Young performers can therefore begin to adapt the movement to different conditions. Feedback is clearly important during this phase to help performers distinguish between correct and incorrect movements. However, it should sometimes be slightly delayed to encourage performers to start trying to correct errors on their own. Young performers will find it easier to respond to feedback from the coach at this stage.

Young performers who have mastered the full movement pattern can progress to the third stage of learning. Movements at this stage will be more consistent, dynamic and fluent. Little cognitive input is required at this stage. Instead the movement of the body, limbs and muscles appears to come naturally and automatically. This enables the young performer's attention to be focused on other aspects such as tactical awareness, changing environments and adaptations. The performer is prepared to learn how to link the fundamental movement patterns together in sport-specific movements. At this stage, feedback should be slightly delayed to give performers the opportunity to reflect on their performance and it is hoped performers can correct their own errors without always relying on feedback.

## The value of feedback

Performers can learn and develop their skills more quickly if they are able to respond to appropriate feedback from themselves or others (usually the coach).

All people, including young performers, are limited in the number of pieces of information they can concentrate on and use at any one time. Giving too much information may confuse and hinder the learning of a movement or prevent the young performer from concentrating on the movement at all – often referred to as *paralysis by analysis*. This is particularly true for young performers in the first stage of learning as the movement is new and requires a great deal of deliberate thinking. Coaches should therefore ensure feedback contains important information, but does not overload performers (ie one or two points at a time). As a performer progresses, the feedback can become more detailed and specific as the movement has become more automatic. Coaches should also encourage young performers to use their own senses (kinaesthetic, visual, auditory) to provide intrinsic feedback as this will encourage them to become more independent.

Young performers also tend to be sensitive to non-constructive criticism. If they are told they are not good at something, they will believe it. Coaches should avoid being judgemental but focus on what should be improved and how it can be improved. They should also make a point of praising the positive aspects related to improvement (make sure the praise is limited and only given if improvement is apparent, otherwise its meaning is devalued). Any constructive criticism should be given between praising positive aspects of performance and directed towards the performance, rather than the young performers themselves. This helps them to keep positive and motivated.

When giving feedback to performers, consider their stage of learning. Some guidelines are given in Table 12 on page 63 to help you give appropriate feedback to young performers. They may need to be adjusted according to the individual needs of the young performer.

*Table 12: Guidelines for giving young performers appropriate feedback*
*KEY  ✓✓ = essential   ✓ = desirable*

| Type of Feedback – Guidelines for Coaches | Recommended for Stage One | Recommended for Stage Two | Recommended for Stage Three |
|---|---|---|---|
| Be positive | ✓✓ | ✓✓ | ✓✓ |
| Praise improvement NB  Only give praise where praise is due | ✓✓ | ✓✓ | ✓✓ |
| Be non-judgemental | ✓✓ | ✓✓ | ✓✓ |
| Give a general idea of the task | ✓✓ | | |
| Use demonstration | ✓✓ | ✓ | ✓ |
| Do not overload – limit corrective feedback to one or two points | ✓✓ | ✓ | ✓ |
| Emphasise the process, not the outcome | ✓✓ | ✓ | |
| Give immediate feedback | ✓✓ | | |
| Do not give feedback too soon – encourage performers to analyse their own performance | | ✓ | ✓✓ |

## 5.3    Sport-specific Movements

After the age of about seven years, children will tend to learn sport-specific movements. Clearly, some performers (eg gymnasts) will learn sport-specific movements even earlier, but they must still learn fundamental movement patterns prior to this. This is because more complex sport-specific movements involve more thought and if performers are preoccupied with coordinating a fundamental movement, they will be distracted from learning the more advanced movements.

Sport-specific movements involve a number of different aspects. Firstly, they may involve the linking together of two or more fundamental movements. For example, the basketball lay-up shot involves running, a jump and a throw in a specific direction. Secondly, they need careful timing. When developing fundamental movements, young performers usually have no time limit to execute the movement and only have the timing of the movement itself to cope with, not additional segments. Using the same example, the lay-up shot requires the timing of the run, jump and finally the shot in order to achieve the outcome. Finally, young performers must be able to adapt these movements to competitive or game situations where the environment is continually changing. The successful acquisition of a sport-specific movement is dependent on whether it can be replicated under conditions of competition and pressure. For example, executing a lay-up shot in practice is commendable, but it has far more worth if it can be replicated during a game, with a full defence and from different angles.

Young performers, as well as adults, are likely to progress through the same three stages of learning (as explained above) to acquire sport-specific movements.

The types of practices relevant for each stage of learning are explained in Chapter 5.4.

As sport-specific movements are being learnt, coaches should encourage young performers to use these in competitive situations. In some sports (eg hockey, football), competitive games are used in practice to help young performers learn sport-specific movements in the context of the sport. However, this is not the case in more technical sports (eg athletics) and coaches should therefore try to ensure performers have the opportunity to try out new skills in practice competitions first – this will help them to build their confidence prior to real competitive situations.

Examples of practices where specific movements for competition can be learnt are:

- practice matches/races (eg 5-a-side games, competitive time trials)

- practice matches/races using skill contingent scoring (ie children score points by successful completion/ demonstration of skill, as opposed to traditional scoring)

- practices which involve set play (eg taking a corner kick in football).

## 5.4 Types of Practice

To provide the best form of practice[1] for young performers, coaches must know how to structure sessions in which learning is accelerated and forgetting is minimised. The specific aims and needs of young performers should form the basis of all sessions. This includes knowing the different stages of learning young performers are going through as well as their short- and long-term goals. Coaches need to decide which practices are most appropriate for their young performers, bearing in mind all the situational factors. Types of practice include:

- whole/part
- blocked/random
- constant/variable
- massed/distributed.

### Whole/part

When adapting a movement or putting some movements together, it is often useful for the coach to explain and demonstrate the movements in terms of the whole-part-whole method. This is particularly relevant to young performers in the first two stages of learning (Chapter 5.2).

Learning by the whole-part-whole method enables the young performer to see firstly the complete movement, then the movement broken down into its fundamental parts, and lastly the complete movement again when all the parts have been sequenced together. Although this method is generally suitable, it may not work so well where the:

- component parts of the technique need to be executed simultaneously
- parts interact closely
- whole technique must be performed rapidly (eg a complex tumbling technique in gymnastics, in which the action of the arms, legs, trunk and head must take place at the same time).

In the example above, it is the correct and smooth coordination of the parts that is essential to the skilful execution of the technique. Dividing the technique interrupts the timing and can result in poor performance. These types of techniques, however complex, are often best coached and practised as a whole action.

---

1   For more information, you are recommended to attend the **scUK** workshop *Improving Practices and Skill* and read its accompanying resource (complimentary with the workshop). All **scUK** resources are available from **Coachwise 1st4sport** (tel 0113-201 5555 or visit www.1st4sport.com).

## Blocked/random

Blocked practice is a series of repetitions of the same movement. While the movements appear the same, they may in fact vary slightly (eg in terms of kicking to different places or with different spin or pace). Coaches should provide short breaks between each practice block to enable them to give performers relevant feedback (if appropriate), allow the performers time to reflect on their own feedback and give them time to recover. Blocked practice is best suited to young performers involved in the very early development of fundamental movements and may be less relevant for those in the autonomous phase of development. It is a very efficient way for young performers to improve and practise. The drawback is that it is not as efficient for helping young performers recall or remember a specific movement in a game situation or at a later time.

Random practice better enables young performers to remember the movements they have learnt and allows for a number of aspects of the sport or game to be practised at once. It may involve a small block of practice on the desired movement pattern, followed by some time spent on a variety of other different but relevant movements before returning

to the initial movement pattern. For example, tennis players who want to practise their serve would first practise a few serves, then practise some volleys and forehands before returning to the serve. This improves performers' retention of certain movements because they must continually recall the information from memory. Random practice is particularly suitable for young performers who are at or near the autonomous phase of learning, and who need refinement and adaptation to competitive situations.

## Constant/variable

Constant practice is where performers repeatedly execute one specific technique (eg attempting to kick every ball with the same leg in the same way every time). It is similar to blocked practice; the difference between the two is that blocked practice allows a degree of variation (eg the way the ball is kicked may vary), whereas in constant practice, the technique is very specific (eg the ball must be kicked in the same way to the same place every time).

Variable practice, however, is where performers deliberately try to vary the execution of one technique. Like random practice, variable practice helps young performers to learn the technique very effectively. This more realistic situation helps the transfer of the technique into the competitive situation and improves recall and long-term retention.

Coaches should encourage variable practice within their sessions for young performers, although it should be used more sparingly with beginners, those in the first stage of learning or those whose confidence or motivation is low. This is because it is harder than constant practice, errors are more likely to occur and this may have a negative effect on performers.

## Massed/distributed

Practice is described as massed when the rest interval between practices is short or non-existent. Conversely, distributed practice provides more frequent and longer rest intervals between practice periods. Massed practice produces more rapid gains although retention may not be as high and young performers may well not be able to cope with the demands both physically and emotionally.

## 5.5    Modifying Sports

Coaches should be aware of the tremendous benefits of modifying sports for young performers. They should know how to adapt the sport to accommodate the physical needs of young performers and maximise learning. Modifications can provide young performers with the opportunities to learn, enjoy and master the necessary skills of the sport in an environment which is suitable for their maturity level and body size, and without any hindrance afforded by game dimensions and equipment.

The benefits of modifying rules (Chapter 3.10) and accommodating young performers' physical needs (Chapter 4.6) have been introduced earlier in this resource. Table 13 on page 68 shows all the possible ways coaches can modify sports to enhance learning. It emphasises how sport can be structured to suit the specific needs of young performers, including their developmental, chronological and training age.

*Table 13: Recommendations for modifying sport*

| Modification | Recommendation |
| --- | --- |
| Playing area | This should steadily increase in line with age to match the increase in physical size and skill level<br><br>Progression must be contingent on skill acquisition and development of new skills required by larger pitch/field/distance |
| Equipment | Equipment should be scaled down to accommodate smaller body proportions<br><br>It should enable young performers to coordinate, develop and master the necessary sport-related movement patterns without being inhibited by heavy or over-sized equipment<br><br>It can be slowly adapted as young performers grow and develop physically so that learning is still being maximised while the equipment demands of the full game are gradually introduced |
| Rules and regulations | Consider developmental age when establishing rules<br><br>Aim to provide young children and beginners, who probably have less fully developed basic movements, with simple rules to give the game shape but no complex restrictions<br><br>Games should be tactically simple (eg target, net/wall, fielding/run scoring), before introducing activities which require more complex strategies (invasion, defending) |
| Group size and structure | Group size should mirror pitch size/equipment changes<br><br>Make sure group size for the activity enables young performers to appreciate the appropriate tactics and skills required when working in groups |

Key strategies for modifying games and activities:

- Keep a note of young performers' progress (eg when they are ready/mature enough for heavier equipment, larger playing area, more complex rules).

- As young performers vary in their rates of development, some of them may need more modifications than others within the same group (eg they may be able to cope with the same playing area and rules but need a lighter racket than the others).

- When developing the rules, keep them very simple at first but give young performers the opportunity to discover more advanced rules for themselves. This encourages them to understand the reasons for rules and fair play. Help them to progress by stopping the practice at appropriate times to ask questions such as 'What if ...?', 'How would you ...?'.

## 5.6 Summary

Coaches should be aware of how young performers learn skills and movement patterns. They should be able to design appropriate practices to maximise the learning of fundamental and sport-specific movements. The use of feedback and different types of practice are crucial for the learning and retention of these movements.

In addition to structuring the practice correctly and providing appropriate feedback, a coach can use the following key strategies to facilitate learning and enjoyment:

- Avoid telling young performers their movement is wrong. This can undermine their confidence and reduce their perceived competence at the activity. Tell them what is right or what they can do to improve their movement.

- When providing task-related information, focus on the *how* and *why* of the action rather than merely the *what.*

- Encourage young performers to tell you what they think, ask you questions about the task and ask themselves questions as they practise.

# CHAPTER SIX:
## Talent Identification and Young Elite Performers

The task of identifying a potential elite performer is a difficult one. There are many factors involved and a young performer who appears to have the potential for the highest level of competition may not necessarily have all the required attributes. Coaches must be careful not to raise unrealistic expectations in their young performers as very few will ever reach the pinnacle of their sport. This chapter introduces how talent is identified and how coaching can be modified to suit the particular needs of young elite performers.

By the end of this chapter, you should be able to:

- identify the key indicators of potential elite performers

- list and explain the special requirements of young elite performers

- structure your coaching to suit the individual needs, goals and abilities of young elite performers.

## 6.0   Are Elite Performers Born or Made?

The nature versus nurture argument suggests that one or the other of these factors is dominant in determining elite performance. The most informed coaches will recognise that both aspects contribute towards success at elite level. The importance of having the innate ability to coordinate and execute movements, to excel in running, throwing or jumping cannot be denied. These natural talents are significant factors in achieving success at a high level.

However, possessing natural ability will not necessarily make a champion. Some performers may clearly be very talented, but without a commitment to training and preparation, they are unable to compete at elite level. Conversely, other less talented performers may achieve high levels because they may be more able to work harder to account for their lack of skill.

Coaches have a key role to play in developing young talented performers into elite performers. They need to be able to identify those performers who have natural ability, and develop their skills and talents so they can compete at the highest level. They should be aware, however, that even the best coaches will not be successful in producing elite performers if they do not have the necessary raw materials. Coaches should therefore focus on maximising the potential of all their performers and appreciate that some may not progress as anticipated.

Once potential elite performers are recognised, coaches have an enormous responsibility to help them set and attain appropriate goals through a structured training programme. Sometimes it may be necessary for coaches to recognise the need to pass a talented young performer on to another coach whose style, expertise and background is more suitable for the development of an elite performer. This may occur, for example, when the performer is moving from the junior to the senior ranks as a different emphasis is required.

## 6.1    Talent Identification

It is helpful for coaches to look at the three different characteristics or features that a young performer must have to reach the highest level in sport. These characteristics, identified by Stojan (1996), are:

- movement talent

- coordination talent

- competition talent.

## Movement talent

Movement talent is the young performer's ability to learn and execute sports movements and correct any errors. It refers to the quality of the movement when observed by a trained eye. Coaches should ask themselves whether movements are efficient and whether the young performer, when given an instruction, can change that movement effectively. If a movement generally conforms to accepted technique and performers have success using that technique, then it is likely the movement is right for them. Clearly, not all successful performers will have textbook movements but these are usually exceptions to the rule. Movement talent is to some extent trainable. The quality of the movement is dependent firstly on mastering the necessary fundamental movement patterns, secondly on the opportunity to practise sport-specific movements and thirdly on the degree of experience in the sport.

## Coordination talent

Coordination talent is a young performer's innate ability to time and execute movements efficiently. It is linked to hand-eye coordination or kinaesthetic awareness (ie how well performers are able to judge the position and movement of their limbs). This talent (often referred to as perceptual-motor ability) is related differently to different sports. For example, in tennis it is called *having a feel for the ball,* in football *having vision* and in swimming, *having a feel for the water.*

Innate coordination is difficult to identify. While a movement may appear to be textbook, mistakes or errors may still occur because of a lack of coordination in some part of the movement. Coaches can use methods such as slow motion video analysis to help them identify the timing and positioning of errors[1]. While specific drills and practices can certainly improve coordination, true coordination talent is mostly innate and will be a great determining factor in the quality of the sport-specific movements.

## Competition talent

Competition talent is the ability of young performers to combine their skills with positive mental resolve and good decision-making in competition. Some believe it is innate in some respects (ie a person may be better able to cope with stressful situations) but there is also no doubt that it can be nurtured and trained. Coaches have a responsibility to provide practices which will mirror as closely as possible the demands of competition in their given sport. This will encourage young performers to use what they have learnt in a high pressure situation and make the right decisions in competition. An example of a competition practice from athletics would be a timed 800m practice race, where the performer races against other athletes.

## Physical talent

In addition to skill-related aspects of performance, body types and physical abilities will also contribute to success in sport. Body types and height tend to influence the types of activity that young performers select and in which they experience success.

---

1    For more information on video analysis, you are recommended to attend the **scUK** workshop *Observation, Analysis and Video* and read its accompanying resource (complimentary with the workshop). All **scUK** resources are available from **Coachwise 1st4sport** (tel 0113-201 5555 or visit www.1st4sport.com).

For example, weightlifters tend to be short with a stocky build while basketball and volleyball players tend to be taller and leaner.

There are also innate physical attributes which are particularly relevant to sports where speed, strength or endurance are essential for success. For example, sports requiring sprint running (eg 100m, hurdles) will require a high degree of speed and strength (power), while cross-country skiing or rowing require high levels of endurance and strength. There are genetic components to all of these aspects and few performers will have the necessary physical attributes required for success at elite level. Most performers will be lucky if they possess even one or two of these attributes.

Physical talent has implications for event and even sport selection. For example, a coach may observe that a long-distance swimmer, while competent, has far greater potential as a sprinter. The swimmer may have the necessary natural speed to be highly successful at sprinting but not the aerobic power to perform at elite level in an endurance event. Just because a person is talented at one sport does not mean they will automatically choose that sport. The coach can therefore assist young performers by pointing out the areas in which their talents could be best put to use.

There are many available methods to test for physical or physiological talents. These range from very expensive laboratory-based tests to simple easy-to-use field tests[1]. Few coaches have access to laboratory testing and instead rely on simple field tests to enable them to assess where the talents of their performers lie. If a talented individual is identified through such tests, many governing bodies have sports science support programmes which may assist in further evaluation once the talented young performer has been identified.

## TASK

Devise a practice which simulates a competitive situation to assess the competitive qualities of a young performer. Remember the practice must test some element of the sport that you would want to see your performer use in competition.

---

1   For more information, you are recommended to attend the **scUK** workshop *Field-based Fitness Testing* and read its accompanying resource *A Guide to Field-based Fitness Testing* (complimentary with the workshop). All **scUK** resources are available from **Coachwise 1st4sport** (tel 0113-201 5555 or visit www.1st4sport.com).

Identifying a talented performer is difficult simply because there are so many factors involved. Just because performers appear talented and are successful for their age, does not necessarily mean they will be champions or high level performers when they become adults. It is possible their performance may be related to an advanced developmental age or years of good practice, experience and guidance.

For example, you may be influenced into thinking some players are more talented than others when in fact their performance is only more successful because they have had a good coach and far more practice/competitive opportunities than others. Coaches should be careful not to raise the expectations of talented young performers by telling them how good they are likely to be. This could result in them feeling that they are a failure if they do not meet the standard they or their coach expect. It may also affect their motivation to participate and they may even drop out of the sport. The following questions may assist coaches in dealing with talent identification.

- Can the performer listen to the coach, watch a demonstration and immediately correct errors or adapt the movement accordingly?

- Observe the performers carefully in practice and competition – are they able to execute movements on their own and adapt to the pressures of competition?

- Use slow motion video replay to identify strengths and weaknesses – use this to build on strengths and correct errors – are performers able to correct these errors when instructed?

- Is the performer consistently more successful than others of a similar developmental age?

- Does the performer demonstrate a constant need to achieve in competition?

- Does the performer possess mental toughness in competition and a positive approach towards achieving goals?

- Is the performer able to cope well with an unsuccessful attempt or competitive experience, and make an effort to learn from mistakes?

While not a definitive guide, a *yes* response to the questions above might indicate that the young performer is talented enough to reach a high level of competition. The coach has a role to provide more advanced training, practice and development programmes for these performers to assist their progression to the highest level.

## 6.2 Setting Goals for Young Elite Performers

Goal-setting for potential or established elite performers is particularly important. Many of the principles outlined in Chapter 3.2 will also apply to young elite performers but there are some additional considerations. Coaches need to help their young elite performers select appropriate goals and accomplish them, bearing in mind they have more potential and ambition than other performers of the same age. These goals should be mutually agreed by the coach and the performer. Input from both parties will give the goals more meaning and they will therefore be more motivating. In addition, coaches should make every effort to inform and, if possible, include the parents of young elite performers in the goal-setting process. This will help them to feel more involved with their children's progress. It will give them a better understanding of what their children are aiming to achieve and how they can best encourage them. Involving the parents in this way should also prevent them from creating conflicting goals which could cause problems (eg when the parents might have higher aspirations than their child).

Often coaches can get very excited when they have talented performers and sometimes they can be too keen for them to make it to the top of their sport. They need to recognise that only a handful of performers ever make it to the highest levels in sport and should therefore not put undue expectations on their young performers. Young elite performers have similar personal needs to others their own age (eg school work, friends, family and other hobbies) and they may or may not be prepared to sacrifice these for success in their sport. Some performers simply may not want to commit the amount of time required to reach the highest level and a coach should respect this and help them set the goals which will maximise performance on the time they are prepared to commit. Coaches should be open and tell their performers of the commitment required for success at elite level – this then gives them the opportunity to make the decisions for themselves.

## Setting the Right Goals

Coaches should encourage young elite performers to set both short- and long-term goals (Chapter 3.2). Any performer needs a sense of immediacy in order to keep focused and motivated in day-to-day practice and training.

Short-term or process goals will help to reduce fluctuations in motivation by giving the performer something to work towards in the near future. Obviously a long-term or ultimate goal is important as it represents the final culmination of the training and practice programme.

## Evaluation

After each set target has passed, coaches and young elite performers need to agree whether goals were achieved or not. This will help them to decide if new targets need to be set or previously set goals need to be changed. It is important for this discussion to be two-way as sports performance is dictated by so many factors. Sometimes factors unknown to the coach or the performer may have affected the outcome of the goal or they may have been over- or under-ambitious. In addition, coaches and performers will also need to evaluate briefly each session to help confirm progress and plan for future sessions.

In summary, coaches should be aware of the need to tailor goals to help elite athletes maximise their talents and performances. It is important for coaches and performers to agree short- and long-term goals. Coaches should encourage parents to be involved in this process. Goals should be written on a calendar programme and be visible to both the performer and coach. Coaches and performers should also set aims for each training or practice session so they are clear on the purpose of each session and how it can lead to achieving ultimate goals.

## 6.3    How Much Should Young Performers Train or Practise?

The young elite performer is likely to be far more skilled and competent at a sport for a given age and this usually means that more advanced training needs to be introduced earlier. However, just because performers are very proficient and have reached a certain age does not mean they should automatically progress to increased amount and types of training. The demands of different sports at elite level will influence the appropriate amount of training and practice for young performers at different stages of development – the coach should make a valued assessment based on each individual performer. This should be done by talking to performers, and explaining how and why changes should be made to training and practice. Performers must agree they are happy to commit to new workloads before any changes take place. Good coaches will plan for these changes in advance.

A specific knowledge of their sport and the demands of training for that sport is necessary for coaches to determine the amount of time and volume of training or practice for a young elite performer. Coaches should be proactive in gaining information regarding current training practices and the preparation time required for high level performances. In addition, they should not regard the practices of others as necessarily the best method for themselves and their performers. Instead, they should adapt new and existing knowledge to suit their own coaching style and the needs of their performers.

In coaching young elite performers, the onus is on coaches to find out if there are any age-related training guidelines in their given sport. Sports science is constantly producing new information[1] which helps coaches of young performers keep up to date with training, practice and preparation for performance trends in their sport.

The programme for young elite performers should help them to achieve their goals. If this is unrealistic, performers may well be disappointed and lose motivation. In some cases, too much training may even lead to damaging physical effects such as

## Three steps to determine the appropriate volume of training and practice for young elite performers

Coaches should:

- discuss and agree goals with their performers or team (including parents) – these should take into account factors such as ability, ambitions, commitment and lifestyle

- match the volume and intensity of training with the goals set and check it is appropriate for the developmental and training age of the performers – is the training programme likely to result in the performers meeting their goals?

- discuss any mismatch with their performers or team – regularly evaluate goals and agree any changes to existing goals or programmes.

---

1   For more information on sports science, you are recommended to subscribe to **scUK**'s technical journal (FHS) and information update service for coaches (**sports coach update**) – see page 84 for details.

extreme fatigue and possible injury. It may also have serious psychological effects which could result in a loss of interest or withdrawal (often termed *burnout* in young performers) from the sport altogether. This emphasises how important it is for the volume and intensity of training to match the performer's goals and commitment to their sport. Coaches should also ensure their performers can commit themselves to the volume and time allocated to training.

## 6.4   Other Issues

While many special requirements of young elite performers have already been introduced, there are some other issues coaches should consider. These include developmental factors, school demands and the ethos of being an elite performer.

## Developmental factors

Increasingly at elite level, developmental factors (physical, psychological and social) influence the motivation, commitment and ultimately performance of young elite athletes. For instance, some talented performers may be very dedicated to their sport when they are young, but as they mature they discover other ambitions and interests (eg hobbies, other sports). Alternatively, they may suddenly improve as a result of physical maturity (eg gains in strength and power). Coaches should be aware of the effects of development on young elite performers and adapt goals and training programmes/ practices accordingly.

## School demands

Young elite performers, whatever their commitment to their sport, are likely to be involved in full-time education and coaches should therefore try to ensure that practices and competitions complement the school year (eg competitions at weekends or during holiday periods, training before or after school). However, it may sometimes be necessary for young elite performers to give priority to their sport (eg if they have the opportunity to compete for their country and gain international experience). Before coaches can advise performers in their best interests, they need to know what constitutes a suitable balance between school and sport for their performers.

They will need to know the answers to questions such as:

- Do the performers want/need qualifications other than sport – do they have ambitions after sport, do they want to go to university?

- Do performers find schoolwork easy or do they have to work very hard?

- How ambitious are performers to excel in sport? How important are sport and education to them?

- What are the performers' chances of making a living from their sport?

- How much will the education of performers suffer if they have to take some time out from school?

To find the answers to these questions, coaches will probably need to discuss them with performers, their parents and a member of staff from their school. Liaison with parents is usually very helpful – they can often provide a good indication of the ideal balance between schoolwork, rest (pleasure) and sport for their children.

Coaches should also make a note of important events such as school exams. Exams are stressful and likely to adversely affect young elite performers' physical and mental capabilities to cope with demanding training sessions (and vice versa). Coaches should therefore try to avoid intensive training during exam periods, and the length and frequency of sessions may need to be reduced.

## Striking a balance

Coaches need to take young performers' sporting, academic and social commitments into account when planning their coaching programmes. A useful starting point is to map out known commitments over a six- or twelve-month period along the lines of Table 14 on page 80.

*Table 14: Junior athlete education planning chart*

| Area | Sept | Oct | Nov | Dec | Jan | Feb |
|---|---|---|---|---|---|---|
| **Competitions** | 4 x club meets | 2 x club meets 1 x regional | 2 x club meets | 1 x regional 1 x national | | |
| **Training** | Thurs/ Sat/Tues | Thurs/ Sat/Tues | Thurs/ Sat/Tues | Regional camp 1st w/end | | National trials |
| **Academic** | | 1st assign't due end of Wk 2 | | 2nd assign't due end of Wk 1 | ← Mock GCSEs → | |
| **Social** | | My birthday on 13th | | Xmas at Grandma's in Ireland | | |
| **Potential hot spots** | | Homework timetable | | Leaving Friday lunchtimes | | **BIG CLASH!!!** |

*Reproduced with the kind permission of the Youth Sport Trust*

This valuable planning tool is used within the Youth Sport Trust's Junior Athlete Education Programme for talented pupils in schools. After completing a Talented Individual Needs Analysis (TINA), each young performer works with his or her coach, parents and teachers (known collectively as *Team You*) to identify key events within a specific time period. In doing so, potential hotspots or clashes can be highlighted as early as possible and all members of *Team You* are made aware of all aspects of the young performer's life.

## The ethos of a young elite performer

Coaches should encourage young elite performers to learn as much as possible from their coach (eg by asking questions if they are unsure or need more information). This should not result in undue reliance on the coach, rather they should see the coach as someone who can assist them in achieving their goals in sport. Coaches should try to help young elite performers to recognise the value of their sport and each training or practice session.

Asking them questions such as 'Do you know why are you doing this practice?' will help them to do this.

In addition, coaches should advise young elite performers to watch and learn from others as well as themselves. There are many lessons to be learned from champions in all sports – the ingredients of elite performers are often very similar, regardless of sport-specific talent and skill. Champions in most sports are extremely dedicated to training, single-minded, positive and most importantly have a real passion for their sport.

## 6.5 Summary

Coaches have a difficult task in identifying talented young performers. There are different types of talent and each affects the performer's overall ability to compete at the highest level. Very few individuals have movement, coordination and competition talents as well as the physical ability to attain elite level. Talent alone can only take a young performer so far. Coaches play a vital role in the planning and development of young elite performers. They need to help them set appropriate goals, and plan a programme to help them attain their goals. Coaches should not lose sight of the fact that young elite performers also have other

commitments just like any other child and adapt the training and practice schedule accordingly. However, they should also recognise when young performers have exceptional talent and ambition, and advise them appropriately so they are able to flourish and become champions.

actionplus

# CHAPTER SEVEN:
# Conclusion

Coaching young performers can be extremely rewarding and enjoyable, as they are usually quick to learn and very enthusiastic. It is important coaches are clear on their philosophy towards young performers and recognise their special requirements. In particular, young performers need the coach to help them balance their sport with all their other commitments and activities.

Young performers have a number of different motives for taking part in sport. Coaches should know what these are so they can help young performers to set realistic goals and structure sessions which are enjoyable as well as productive.

By understanding how young performers develop physically, coaches will be able to modify sessions according to their developmental stage and gradually increase the physical demands of sport as they mature. Young performers also need guidance on training principles and safe practice as they are more susceptible to certain illnesses and injuries than adults.

Coaches should know how young performers acquire skill at different stages of development and learning so they can help them to progress. The appropriate use of feedback and practice is crucial for the learning and retention of skill in sport.

Finally, some young performers will be more talented and ambitious than others. It is important that coaches can identify these performers and structure sessions so they are able to excel at their sport. Most importantly, coaches should aim to help all young performers achieve their goals, however big or small, and ensure their experiences of sport are positive and fun.

## Where Next?

This handbook was written to help coaches develop their skills for coaching young performers. To help put some of the ideas into practice, you are strongly recommended to reread any of the chapters that are particularly relevant to you and your performers. Take note of those workshops and resources recommended throughout the book. These will help to extend your knowledge further on specific topics and improve your coaching.

Recommended **scUK** workshops and resources (complimentary with the corresponding workshop) include:

| scUK Develop Your Coaching Workshop | Accompanying Resource |
| --- | --- |
| A Guide to Mentoring Sports Coaches | A Guide to Mentoring Sports Coaches |
| Analysing your Coaching | Analysing your Coaching |
| Coaching and the Law | – |
| Coaching Children and Young People | Coaching Young Performers |
| Coaching Disabled Performers | Coaching Disabled Performers |
| Coaching Methods and Communication | The Successful Coach |
| Creating a Safe Coaching Environment | Creating a Safe Coaching Environment |
| Developing Power and Speed | – |
| Equity in Your Coaching | Equity in Your Coaching |
| Field Based Fitness Testing | A Guide to Field Based Fitness Testing |
| Fitness and Training | Physiology and Performance |
| Fuelling Performers | Fuelling Performers |
| Goal-setting and Planning | Planning Coaching Programmes |
| Good Practice and Child Protection | Protecting Children |
| Imagery Training | Imagery Training |
| Improving Practices and Skill | Improving Practices and Skill |
| Injury Prevention and Management | Sports Injury |
| Introduction to Core Stability | – |
| Motivation and Mental Toughness | Motivation and Mental Toughness |
| Observation, Analysis and Video | Observation, Analysis and Video |
| Performance Profiling | Performance Profiling |
| The Responsible Sports Coach | – |
| Understanding Eating Disorders | – |

All **scUK** resources are available from:

**Coachwise 1st4sport**
Coachwise Ltd
Chelsea Close
Off Amberley Road
Armley
Leeds
LS12 4HP
Tel: 0113-201 5555 Fax: 0113-231 9606
Email: enquiries@1st4sport.com Website: www.1st4sport.com

**scUK** also produces a technical journal, *Faster, Higher, Stronger (FHS)* and an information update service for coaches (**sports coach update**). Details of these services are available from:

**sports coach UK**
114 Cardigan Road
Headingley
Leeds
LS6 3BJ
Tel: 0113-274 4802
Fax: 0113-275 5019
Email: coaching@sportscoachuk.org
Website: www.sportscoachuk.org

For further details of **scUK** workshops in your area, contact the **scUK** Business Support Centre (BSC).

**sports coach UK** Business Support Centre
Sport Development Centre
Loughborough University
Loughborough
Leicestershire LE11 3TU

Email: bsc@sportscoachuk.org

# References

Allert, L (1996) **The Swedish sports secondary schools' programme: a report to the Swedish Sports Confederation**

Ames, C (1992) **Achievement goals, motivational climate and motivational processes.** In: GC Roberts (ed) *Motivation in sport and exercise.* Champaign IL, Human Kinetics, pp 161–176. ISBN 0 87322 876 6

Bloom, BS (1985) **Developing talent in young people.** New York, Ballantine Books. ISBN 0 345319 51 6

Cote, J (1999) **The influence of the family in the development of talent in sport.** *Sports Psychologist.* Vol 13

Ericsson, KA and Charness, N (1994) **Expert performance.** *Am Psych.* 49(8), pp725–747

Gallahue, DL and Ozmun, JC (1997) **Understanding motor development.** Madison, WC Brown. ISBN 0 697294 87 0

Harsanyi, L (1990) **Az edzes egy even belui szakaszai.** Budapest, OTSH

Lawn Tennis Association (1997) **Coaching junior players.** Leeds, Coachwise Business Solutions/The National Coaching Foundation. ISBN 0 947850 40 6

Stojan, S (1996) **From talent to champion – the role of the coach.** *Coaching Excellence.* No 14, pp3, 6–7

Wilmore, JH and Costill, DL (1999) **Physiology of sport and exercise.** Champaign IL, Human Kinetics. ISBN 0 73600 084 4

Youth Sport Trust (2001) **Young athlete handbook.** Champaign IL, Human Kinetics. ISBN 0 7360 3712 8

# Further Reading

Balyi, I (2002) **Long-term athlete development – the system and solutions.** *Faster, Higher, Stronger (FHS)* Issue 14, pp6–9. For copies, tel 0113-290 7612.

Lee, M (1993) **Coaching children in sport: principles and practice.** London, E & FN Spon. ISBN 0 419 18250 0

Stafford, I (2005) **Coaching for Long-term Athlete Development.** Leeds, Coachwise Business Solutions/The National Coaching Foundation. ISBN 1 902523 70 9